THE WRONG WAY

Millennial Mind Publishing
An imprint of American Book Publishing
American Book Publishing
P.O. Box 65624
Salt Lake City, UT 84165
www.american-book.com
Printed in the United States of America on acid-free paper.

The Wrong Way

Designed by Bethann Santry, design@american-book.com

Publisher's Note: *This publication is designed to provide accurate and authoritative information in regard to the subject matter covered. It is sold or distributed with the understanding that the publisher and author is not engaged in rendering legal, accounting, or other professional service. If legal advice or other expert assistance is required, the services of a competent professional person in a consultation capacity should be sought.*

ISBN 1-58982-202-1

Van Drie, Carol J., The Wrong Way

Special Sales

These books are available at special discounts for bulk purchases. Special editions, including personalized covers, excerpts of existing books, and corporate imprints, can be created in large quantities for special needs. For more information e-mail orders@american-book.com, 801-486-8639.

THE WRONG WAY

Carol J. Van Drie

Dedication

This book is dedicated to the man of my dreams, my husband Mark. I am so grateful God gave me the perfect man to grow old with.

Preface

I was a young teenager when I realized Jesus was Lord. For the next seventeen years, I had knowledge of Jesus Christ and knew him as the Savior, but did not make him Lord of my life. I did not give him my *whole* heart. This lack of submission led me on a lifelong search to find what I lacked in my life.

I searched for Jesus in other human beings and human religious organizations. When I married my husband in 1979, I expected him to fill the emptiness inside of me. I believed he would make me whole. As a result, our marriage was rocky in those early years. Immediately after the birth of my first daughter, I felt a renewed need to search for a way to fill the void in my heart. I was not at peace, and fear became my constant companion. I was frightened of everything: flying, driving, aging, and many more things. During this particularly vulnerable time, a family friend introduced me to The Way International. Victor Paul Wierwille was the charismatic founder and I quickly fell into the clutches of this supposed biblically based organization. It was instead, a cult.

What led to my involvement with this mind-warping cult for six long years, as well as my subsequent break from it and ultimate delivery from its brainwashing techniques, is contained within these pages. By my testimony, I hope to warn others of the dangers of looking towards humankind or any religious organization for fulfillment. There is just one man, the Lord Jesus Christ, God in the flesh, who can completely satisfy a longing heart. This can be achieved solely by a personal relationship with him. A life of service, submission, obedience, and trust in God is the exclusive way to true happiness, peace, and joy. It took me most of my life to discover this. My prayer is that my story will lead others to this knowledge. If it stops even one individual from making the same mistakes I made, then my trial will have ended in victory with all the glory going to God.

What you are about to read is the truth to the best of my memory. I have changed most of the names to protect both the innocent and the guilty. It is not my desire to drag names and reputations through the mud just for the sake of doing so. Rather, it is my desire to inform and warn others of the subtle manipulations of the cult The Way International.

Contents

BOOK I

THE WAY IN

Chapter 1

My World of Secrets

If Jesus Christ is God, we have not yet been redeemed.
—Wierwille, *Jesus Christ is not God*

* * * * *

When I was fourteen years old, I began corresponding with a schoolmate who had recently moved from my hometown of Latham, New York (a suburb of Albany) to Syracuse. Debbie soon began changing. Through her letters, I started to realize that she seemed to have her finger on the pulse of what I was looking for: happiness. I wanted to know more about this Jesus her letters spoke of.

I was baptized in the Catholic church and raised Roman Catholic. In all the years of attending church, going to Sunday school, and even attending a private women's Catholic college, I was never taught to read the Bible. Debbie's letters urged me to do so. I started reading and soon felt a sense of peace. Hope filled my heart. I bought a huge sterling cross on a chain and wore it every day, hoping my friends would ask me about it so I could share this exciting new feeling I had. But no one asked. One day, I joined my local buddies in our meeting place in the woods. I fairly burst with news about Jesus, blurting it out even though no one had brought up the subject. My confession was met with an awkward silence. Being an insecure bundle of nerves at the time, and not wishing to alienate myself from my pals, I closed my mouth and never mentioned it again. I took off the cross, stopped reading my Bible, and stepped back into the familiar confines of the Catholic church. Slowly, the new joy I had felt began fading. My life carried on as usual.

* * * * *

In sixth grade, my parents separated and later divorced. As an only child with little family support, I retreated into my world of secrets. No other friends of mine had divorced parents. My mother became a single parent and had to support us on her meager secretary's salary. Even though my precious, widowed grandmother who shared our house as well as the bills took work as a waitress, our finances were strapped. To add to these strains, I was completely wrapped up in a world of placing emphasis on my looks—marginal at best—thus feeding my insecurities further. My father reinforced my inadequacies with his verbally and mentally abusive nature. I do not remember him calling me by my given name until the day I married. I recall many harmless names, but the one that he most frequently used was *dum-dum*.

I tried to keep things a secret: my parents were going through a messy divorce, we were almost eligible for food stamps, and I was a latchkey child. Most of all, I tried to hide how desperately insecure and ugly I felt. I lived in a fabricated world of fantasy through pop music, books (I was a voracious reader), and movies. I was popular, but in a class-clown type of way.

Throughout high school, all of my girlfriends were not just prettier than me…they were gorgeous. At Shaker High School in Colonie, New York, we gained the reputation of having the best-looking guys and gals in the substantially large school district. That is, most everyone at Shaker except me. Although my braces were gone by then, and my glasses gave way to contacts, I just never quite achieved the popularity with the guys that my cheerleader and homecoming queen friends did. My senior year, every one of the girls in my clique was nominated for homecoming queen. I was not.

It seemed, as I always used to say, I couldn't pay a guy to date me. All of my girlfriends had steadies; I had "brothers." One particularly beautiful girlfriend, Chrissy, indirectly (in a manner of speaking) arranged a date for me to our junior prom. Matty managed to show a great interest in me the weeks prior to the prom. We were already great friends, and I always thought him to be absolutely adorable, but he suddenly showed more than a friendly interest in me. He knew I was practically attached at the hip to Chrissy, so a relationship with me meant he could be closer to the true object of his affection: Chrissy. I had spent money I could ill afford on a beautiful pink spaghetti-strap A-line dress, and even had my hair done in an updo with long ringlets in the back. I actually felt a bit confident that I looked lovely. Oblivious to Matty's plan until much later, I went to the junior prom, unaware that my date was drooling all over his pink and white tux the entire fun-filled evening for Chrissy. It was this type of baggage I carried with me into my college years at an exclusive women's institution, Ladycliff College, in Highland Falls, New York.

The summer prior to my first venture away from home witnessed a change in me. I have been blessed, it seems, from birth with a strong singing voice. My range is wide, and this led to my singing lead vocals in rock bands. In those days, during the latter portion of my senior year in high school, as well as in other musical ventures throughout college, I sang for good money. On any given weekend, as pay for a Friday and Saturday night of singing approximately three to five hours, I made up to three hundred dollars depending upon the venue. A cheap, seedy bar only offered about seventy-five dollars for two nights, but a decent club paid three hundred dollars or more for two nights of doing what I loved.

A physical change happened to me as well. I lost weight. Although never terribly heavy, I was not as thin as the current trend dictated. My experience in the band and the positive feedback that resulted made me slightly more confident. Even though my outer shell had matured and become more polished, the inner core still reflected an adolescent package of braces and glasses engulfed in fat.

The interesting fact about Ladycliff College, other than its pristine placement a mere few hundred feet from the gates of the United States Military Academy at West Point, was that it was a Catholic school. Many of the professors were nuns. The atmosphere was open to all faiths, but Catholicism was emphasized, naturally.

One day in my freshman year during one of my philosophy classes, the sister stood before the class and posed this scenario: If Jesus Christ came today, as he had come to the apostles, and we *knew* he was Jesus, would any of us have trouble going with him? Although the content of the whole discussion isn't clear to me today, the immediate reaction of the class is, just as if it happened yesterday. I sat at my desk emphatically shaking my head no, while my remaining classmates nodded their heads yes. What was truly shocking to me was the sister's response (she hadn't noticed my reaction to her question as she commented). "Yes, I too would have a great deal of trouble leaving my family and my teaching profession. I have some possessions that mean a great deal to me, and it would be difficult for me to leave all of those things as well as my loved ones behind."

I was aghast! I would leave everything and follow Christ in a heartbeat! Yet here was a woman well into her sixties, who wasn't even allowed to get married and lead a normal life, essentially saying she wasn't certain of her devotion to God! She had actually come to the conclusion that she wasn't confident she would follow the very man she had spent her entire adult life serving. I realized my search for spiritual fulfillment had begun again and that I would not find my way to God through the Catholic church (as I had begun to suspect long before this moment). Although many have found fulfillment in the Catholic church, I felt it was time for me to search elsewhere. I would have to wait until my senior year for God to manifest himself to me in the physical world.

Chapter 2

Ross Glenn Samson IV

In other words, I am saying that Jesus Christ is not God, but the Son of God. They are not "co-eternal," without beginning or end.
—Wierwille, *Jesus Christ is Not God*

* * * * *

It was 1978. Mark, my husband-to-be, had graduated from West Point, class of 1977. His first assignment was in Fort Lewis, Washington, where he practiced his newly learned lieutenant skills, while I finished my degree in English literature. We were not engaged, but I knew he was "the one," and as he said via long distance telephone conversations, he felt the same about me. My social life consisted of going out with my girlfriends and cadets from West Point, in massive groups. This was how I met Ross Glenn Samson IV.

Ross was in his junior year at the academy, and we instantly became steadfast friends. We hung out together every free moment we had. He made me laugh, and was a heck of a party guy. We had long, long talks on the phone every day. He became my best friend. Since Mark was not committing to me in a tangible way, Ross and I grew extremely close and I freely ran with it. We regularly attended parties together at Bear Mountain, a lodge just a short drive from West Point and neighboring Ladycliff. In the 1970s, the legal drinking age in the state of New York was eighteen. Bear Mountain Lodge had a great bar and rented out conference rooms. Quite often, as a retreat from our studies, a group of us would pool our money and throw a huge party with a few kegs in one of these rooms. Some of the guest rooms on the complex were very inexpensive; it would not be unusual for twenty-five or more of us to crash in one room so we wouldn't have to drive home less than sober. The only way to describe the frenetic pace of college life is to recall the unending stamina and reckless abandon of youth…

Towards the close of Thanksgiving break, I was in the school parking lot unloading my car before classes resumed. Adrian, a mutual friend, approached me saying, "Gee, Carol, I'm so sorry to hear about Ross."

I had no idea what she was talking about.

She proceeded to tell me that Ross had been to a party on Long Island over the holiday. He left on foot around midnight, apparently planning to meet some friends at someone's house. The ground was covered with three inches of freshly fallen snow. He had been drinking an enormous amount of vodka. No one knows exactly what happened, but he evidently took a shortcut down an embankment. He must have slipped, fallen, and then landed unconscious on the railroad tracks. As if that weren't horrific enough, a train came by and hit him, dragging him God only knows how far, before he ended up under an abandoned railway station platform. In the wee hours of the morning, two young men were walking across the field perpendicular to the platform. Ross hadn't made a movement or a sound, but something made one of them turn back. That is how he was found.

Adrian told me Ross was at a Long Island hospital, in a coma, and barely clinging to life. I tried to find the hospital he was in by using the dorm phone, but was unsuccessful. Impulsively, I decided to drive to Long Island and find the hospital. Other than the name of the facility and that it was somewhere on Long Island, I was flying blind. I asked two girlfriends to come with me.

I drove my orange Vega south, and prayed (not something I did often then) for direction. I decided once I arrived in Long Island, I would follow every blue roadside hospital sign, and stop to ask if Ross had been admitted. The very first hospital I found was the one I was looking for!

My adrenaline was in overdrive when I burst through the double swinging doors of the intensive care unit as if I owned the place. My two friends, Janie and Rusty (a petite math wiz and constant college companion, respectively), had to run to keep up with me. A nurse rushed forward, telling us in excited, hushed tones that visiting hours were over and that we had to leave immediately. The ICU had rooms to the right, extending approximately two hundred feet and curving in a horseshoe-like fashion, with a large nurses' station in the center in full view of each room.

I started to cry, begging the nurse to let us see Ross because we had just heard of his accident today, and had driven all the way from Albany. She softened and agreed to let us see him for a few minutes. She started to explain that he had suffered severe head injuries and wouldn't look the same. While she talked, she led us forward. I looked blankly into each Plexiglas room as we walked. They reminded me of little fishbowls: translucent walls of plastic with flimsy pull-curtains for privacy. At the top of the horseshoe-shaped hall, a tiny, elderly man with numerous tubes sticking out of him lay motionless in a bed. We stopped in front of this room. To my utter horror, I realized this old, shriveled up man was Ross. I had never fainted before, but at that moment, I started falling backwards, the ringing in my ears deafening, the sight before me swirling. If it weren't for my girlfriends, I would have hit the floor like a rock. The shock of seeing Ross this way—my crazy, nutty pal—was absolutely overwhelming.

Ross's head was almost entirely covered with heavy bandaging. His face was swollen beyond recognition, as was his unbandaged right arm resting above the sheets. He was on a respirator, and tubes led from his body to numerous other medical apparatuses and back. The maddening swoosh and hiss of the respirator were the only sounds reverberating in the room. This was not the same Ross I had last seen swilling beers at Bear Mountain. This simply could not be the same vital young cadet whom I called my friend.

For the next several weeks, I became obsessed with Ross's recovery. I would make the two-hour, traffic-congested trip to see him almost every day, either after classes, or in between them. I also prayed a great deal and when I say I prayed, I mean I got down on my knees every day and pleaded with God to bring Ross back to life. The doctors said he had little to no chance of recovering, and that if he did make it, he would most likely be a vegetable. I couldn't eat, and slept infrequently. It seemed every waking moment was spent thinking about Ross, praying for him, or visiting him. This went on for over a month.

By Christmas, my friends were becoming impatient with me. I wasn't the happy party girl they were used to, and my days revolved around willing Ross well. I was weak from lack of sleep, and my weight had dropped dramatically. My friends got together in a group—a confrontational type of thing one might do with a drug addict or an alcoholic—and told me about their concern for my well-being. I was touched, but unmoved.

One evening, I decided to go to the chapel and pray for a sign—any sign—to determine if Ross would live or die. I had to know so that I could get on with my life. I decided to confront the God I believed a distant, mysterious being. I was desperate, and he was my last hope.

It was a terribly cold night. At around 10:30 that evening, I climbed the small hill to the tiny chapel as the wind cut through my coat with a vengeance. I opened the heavy double doors and sank into a pew near the center-right of the church. The only light in the room was a solitary candle burning on the altar. I was alone.

I knelt down, crying and praying for at least thirty minutes. I cried out to God, asking him to please show me whether or not I should keep praying for Ross. The doctors and nurses at the hospital, the priests and nuns at school, everyone was telling me to resign myself to the obvious: Ross wasn't going to make it. The fact that he had hung on this long was in and of itself a miracle. I wanted *more* of a miracle. I couldn't accept he would die at such a young age. I just wouldn't allow myself to even think of it. However, I was weary and ready to give up, but only if God himself would tell me to. I felt completely drained and was about to leave for the dorm when I noticed the flame on the lone altar candle start to flicker. Suddenly, it went out. No one came in or out of the chapel.

No windows were open. Only the light from the sidewalk lamps outside illuminated the chapel now as I stood up slowly in awe. For one moment, my heart leapt with hope, but then I realized that an extinguished light probably meant Ross would die.

In a strange way, this gave me peace. I slowly left the pew, and with only one glance back, went out the doors, through the snow, to my dorm room. I told some of the girls what had happened, but they didn't know what to make of it. I knew. God, the great I Am, had deigned to answer my plea that night. I slept soundly for the first time in many weeks.

Chapter 3

Answered Prayers

"When I was a young lad, my mother would say to me on Saturday night before I went to town, 'Be a good boy.' This admonition actually never helped because one cannot make a boy good by telling him to be good. People seldom read the Word of God by being told they have to read it. People never tap the resources of prayer by being told that they ought to pray. I do not tell you that you ought to read the Bible; I teach you *how* to read it. I do not tell you that you ought to pray; I tell you *how* to pray. I do not tell you that you should believe; I teach you *how* to believe."[1]

            —Wierwille, *Power for Abundant Living*

* * * * *

---

[1] PFAL pg. 15

I wasn't able to see Ross the next day, but made the trip the day after. As I entered the ICU doors, one of the regular nurses on duty spotted me and rushed towards me. She grabbed my shoulders and practically shouted, "HE OPENED HIS EYES!" I stood there absolutely astounded.

I had checked the candle early the next morning, and there was plenty of wick and wax left in the cup. I took the extinguishing of the flame to be a clear sign from God that the light of Ross's life would go out as well. I had entered the hospital that day with the resigned notion I would be saying good-bye. This was something quite different indeed.

As I hurriedly walked to Ross's room, the nurse clicked back into her professional mode. She chattered away in my ear that this could be the only level he would reach; opening his eyes didn't necessarily mean a full recovery, and some patients reach this stage and remain that way for years, blah, blah, blah. I knew better. I realized that God had just worked a miracle in Ross Glenn Samson IV, and I was a witness to this awesome fact.

I entered his fishbowl and drew the three privacy curtains to create a "private" room. I called Ross's name as I had done a hundred times before. This time I witnessed the most wonderful sight in the world. Ross sat propped up, and once I called him, his eyes opened. They were unfocused, but OPEN! According to the monitors, he usually responded to the sound of my voice. That morning, despite his eyes remaining unfocused, he started blinking rapidly as I spoke to him. This young man, given up for dead by the entire medical staff, was not only very much alive, but I also knew in my heart he wasn't going to live as an invalid. His right arm had been badly broken, and was still extremely swollen and discolored. Atrophy had started to set in, which is common for head trauma or comatose patients. The doctors had not even set the bones, anticipating his imminent death. They were going to have quite a bit of work ahead of them, putting Ross back together, because he was going to need full use of his limbs!

As the days progressed, I brought things to make his room more personal. Before the accident, he had loved a current hit song that played on the Top 40 radio stations. I brought in a Cassette player and kept it on one of the tables next to his bed. Whenever the song came on during a visit, I would crank up the volume, getting myself in trouble with the ICU nurses, but it consistently got a response from Ross. The monitor showed an increase in his heart rate, and he would open his eyes as if trying to focus, keeping them open the duration of the song. I also brought in his cadet picture and taped it to the wall near his bed. I wanted the nurses and staff to see the *real* Ross, not this person who barely resembled him.

* * * * *

Nearly two weeks later, Ross would not open his eyes no matter what I tried. I was deeply disappointed, and for the first time since that night in the chapel, doubt for his full recovery crept into my mind. I walked out of his room and sat dejectedly on a bench nearby, as one of my friends attempted to console me. Due to my frequent visits, I had come to know a family who visited their father, now in a diabetic coma. This day, his son, Tim, came out holding a Bible. He asked how Ross was and I told him of my concerns. Tim asked if he could pray over Ross. I said sure, and we all went back into Ross's room.

Tim and I stood near Ross's head on the right, and my girlfriends, Janie and Rusty, stood by his left side. Tim opened his Bible, while placing his hand over Ross's hand resting on top of the covers. He bowed his head in prayer. The instant Tim touched Ross's hand, Ross's eyes fluttered open. Tim prayed for at least four or five minutes. Ross's eyes remained open the entire time. When Tim finished, he took his hand from Ross, and only then did Ross slowly close his eyes. Previously, Ross only responded by opening his eyes for a few seconds at a time, then closing them for a few seconds only to open them again a minute or so later if there was audio stimulation. Tears sprang to my eyes and my doubt disappeared. I knew then, no matter what, Ross was going to be all right. By God's might and mercy, Ross would make it.

About a month later, Ross was transferred to a military facility in Texas, where he began the long, tedious road to recovery. I was determined not to let the distance between us interrupt our friendship. I wrote to Ross every single day, willing him to persevere through his physical therapy sessions. I wanted him to feel my presence and know I had not forgotten him, nor had I given up on him.

When he was transferred back to West Point, I reclaimed my position by his side. Ross's recovery was miraculous, but not overnight. There were times he had to face his limitations and it frustrated him immensely. He was used to being in control: the leader, the comforter, and the assured one. However, his persistence to reclaim that persona drove him. I remained a steadfast friend, cheering him on and comforting him in the moments his limitations surmounted his abilities.

Ross made a full recovery. He was a medical miracle and everyone, including his own family, was amazed.

At the time, Ross seemed unmoved by this chain of events. He didn't believe there to be any supernatural cause for his recovery. During one visit I had with him months into his recovery, I told him what a powerful miracle God had worked in his life.

"Carol, I was the one with the strength to get well. God didn't do anything."

His humanistic reply shocked me. I was stunned into silence. He said that while he was in a coma he didn't remember anything, and relied on witnesses like myself who were present during his hospital stay immediately after the accident to relate what had happened to him. Yet he believed he had made *himself* recover. But our God is not one to sit so silently after he has performed such a good work. In time, Ross became aware of God's provision, acknowledging the Gentle Healer for his miraculous recovery. Today, he holds a leadership position in his church: a walking miracle for all to behold.

Regardless of my witnessing these amazing events unfold right before my eyes, I too lacked the humility and wisdom to seek this mighty and merciful God who answered prayer. I did not pursue that path until many years later, during a vulnerable time in my life when I would come to sit in the living room of a family friend. She would introduce me to The Way International, and how I could possess "Power for Abundant Living" through it.

Chapter 4

On German Soil

Lots of stuff I teach is not original. Putting it all together so that it fit—that was the original work. I learned wherever I could, and then I worked that with the Scriptures. What was right on with the Scriptures, I kept; but what wasn't, I dropped.

—Kahler, *The Cult that Snapped*

And many false prophets shall rise, and shall deceive many. And because iniquity shall abound, the love of many shall wax cold.

—Matt. 24:11-12 King James Version

* * * * *

I married Mark on September 1, 1979. From the onset, we were headed for trouble due to my vast emotional needs, which no human could possibly fulfill. I expected Mark to be my everything, and although he was good to me, the task before him was unattainable. My insecurities and emotional highs and lows would test the patience of any husband, no matter how devoted. Mark dutifully became absorbed in the responsibilities of being an army officer to the point that I felt myself slowly fading into the background. I was never able to feel secure in his love or needed in those days, and his complete dedication to the army only made matters worse.

I decided I wanted a baby: someone I could love and who would love me and *need* me. I hounded Mark until he reluctantly agreed.

In 1982, early in my pregnancy, Mark was assigned to Würzburg, Germany. From the moment I arrived, I detested being there. I was thrust into a country very far from home, with different customs and a lingering anti-American sentiment. I am of Italian descent and have an ethnic look about me. At the time, I had long, dark brown hair (now graying), big brown eyes, and a nose much like Cher had before plastic surgery. I never had a problem with my ethnicity. In fact, I take great pride in looking so distinctly like my people. When I was mistaken for a Jew, which happened quite frequently, I didn't mind that either, as my mother's roots are first in Italy, then on Delancy Street, New York City. The two cultures blended so much my mother always told me the line between them was almost blurred.

In Germany, my noticeably non-Aryan appearance found me experiencing racial prejudice for the first time in my life. I was disliked simply for the way I looked. I believe I was generally mistaken for Jewish, and this made my interactions with the German population awkward. For example, I would shop in the Würzburg town square, trying to fit in with the locals by using a basket to shop at the outdoor markets just as they did. I would select my items and go to pay the merchant, usually a blond, blue-eyed man or woman chattering in very cheery, welcoming tones. When it was my turn to pay, the eyes of the clerk would wax cold. I was looked over and greeted with silent stares of disdain, despite my friendly *danke schön*. This treatment wounded me deeply, and I often came home in tears. I was terribly homesick from the moment I set foot on German soil. I missed my mother and grandmother even before leaving the U.S. I longed for my friends back in the States. I couldn't just pick up the phone and call because long distance was horribly expensive, but I did anyway, leading to fights with Mark over our enormous phone bills. I felt Germany as a whole simply did not like me. And the sentiment was greatly returned.

To make matters worse, the housing situation, even for Germans, was a nightmare. We spent two long months together in a hotel when I arrived. In the early 1980's, we did not have access to English speaking TV channels and not having cable was agonizing for me. We didn't even have any clear radio stations. Mark had arrived a month before me to look for a place, but had been completely unsuccessful. Altogether, it took us three months to find a place to live. We searched for a place every single day during our two-month stay at that hotel. It was a frustrating process to say the least.

Several other things made the entire wait for housing virtual torture. For example, I managed to completely humiliate myself at the hotel. I knew a bit of German, but was very shy about using it. Still, I gave it a try during the long days I waited for Mark to come home from work, either while lunching at the hotel restaurant or just asking some general questions at the front desk. Every day, right before lunchtime, I would go to the front desk to call my husband. There were no phones in the room, and this was many years before everyone had a cell phone attached to their ear. I was just beginning to become quite noticeably pregnant, and was so thrilled with my impending motherhood that I found myself constantly rubbing my belly.

The first time I asked to use the phone, I decided to try out my limited command of the German language. I could not for the life of me, even after three years of high school German, remember the German word for *telephone*. As I approached the front desk, I looked at the telephone on the counter and noticed the word *Notruf* right there on the phone. Assuming that this must be the German word I needed, I stood there rubbing my belly, pointing to the phone and asking, *"Notruf, bitte."* I thought I was saying, "Telephone, please."

The front desk clerk, previously sitting on a high stool, nearly fell off attempting to get me the phone across a very deep counter so that I could easily reach it. As I dialed Mark's office, I found myself thinking that perhaps I had judged this country a little too harshly. Look at how accommodating they were with a simple request like a telephone call!

I made this same call, in almost exactly the same manner every single workday, and for the first few weeks, with exactly the same reaction from the person behind the front desk. I approached the desk, usually rubbing my belly, pointing to the phone and saying, *"Notruf, bitte,"* as the front desk person tripped over himself to get me the phone.

One day, while looking for a place to live, Mark and I were driving on the Autobahn (the German superhighway without speed limits), and we came upon a construction site. These sites are very clearly marked well in advance of the construction due to the fact that there is no speed limit and it is literally a matter of life or death. On many of the fast approaching signs was the word *Notruf*. It suddenly occurred to me, in a moment of crystal clear revelation, what a *fool* I had been making of myself. Every day, when asking for the telephone and rubbing my belly, I was pointing to the phone, saying, *"Emergency,* please." At that same moment, I remembered that the German word for telephone was *telefon—pronounced the same as in English.*

The humiliation burned my cheeks. I thought I would die from the shock of it! How could I possibly face the front desk people again? How could I even walk *past* the front desk again without wanting to crawl into the ground and just die from the shame? Sure enough, one day, when coming down the stairs, I heard two women at the desk talking about the "stupid American" who had an "emergency" all the time and when was she going to leave?

Oh, how I *detested* Germany!

* * * * *

We finally found a rental. The place was way out in the country, next to a farm, on the edge of a tiny, ancient German village, a good clip from the army post. The name of the little hamlet was Gerlachshousen. It was early spring, and the town, though beautiful, was isolated. My only close neighbor was an elderly couple, which seemed to comprise the population for that area. We had no television reception, no clear radio stations, and only a tiny hot water tank above the kitchen sink and a slightly larger one for the only bathroom shower. If I wanted fresh air during the hot summer months, I would open my windows to the stench of manure and countless flies. Apparently, window screens had not caught on yet. So essentially, my windows stayed permanently shut during the warm weather months. VCRs and tape rental were not very popular yet, so the library on the army post became my favorite hangout. I must have read four or five novels per week, and wrote *numerous* letters. I was terribly, terribly homesick.

Mark worked long, hard hours and spent quite a bit of time training in field exercises. I literally counted the minutes to his arrival home at 6:00 in the evening. If he was even slightly delayed, I would instantly call his office and whine. I *lived* for him to walk through the door.

The bitter icing on the miserable cake was when the shipment of our household goods came. Most of our possessions were lost, stolen, or destroyed. I spent the whole first year moaning and complaining about it to anyone who would listen. After a while, there weren't too many listeners. I envied other people's belongings. If we visited someone's home and they had nice things, I stewed about it for at least a week, resentfully wondering why *we* weren't so fortunate.

To add to my ever piling woes, the larger I got in my pregnancy—believe me, "beached whale" is a kind description—the more insecure in Mark's love I became. He also seemed more distant due to his workload, and although I expected him to be husband, friend, support, entertainment, and a host of other emotional Band-Aids, he simply couldn't fit the bill. No one could. I missed my mother and grandmother desperately, and knew they wouldn't be able to be present for the birth of our first baby. This, too, caused more undue angst and numerous arguments between Mark and me, since our phone bills continued to be massive. I filled my days with obsessive housekeeping. I dusted, waxed floors, vacuumed, and cleaned bathrooms every day. Other than read and write home, what else was there to do?

Finally, the long-awaited event took place. Amber was born September 1, 1982, our third anniversary. The instant she came into the world, I felt, "Now I know why God put me on this planet." I immediately decided not only would I be the perfect housekeeper, but I was bound to be the most loving, caring mother on earth. I had no idea what the heck I was doing—our family practice doctor, a wonderful, patient, army officer, received numerous frantic phone calls from me—but I was going to do my very best to do this mothering thing right!

During this time, fears started to surface. I knew we would be planning a trip home in the near future to see our family, but the thought of flying terrified me. The Autobahn had no speed limit, and caused me endless apprehension every time I drove on it. I just couldn't imagine anything happening to my precious Amber, which wasn't hard to picture with speeds rivaling the Indy 500.

My figure had changed dramatically. Having never found it necessary to exercise before, the option didn't even come to mind as I painfully viewed my lumpy, distorted, stretch-marked body in a full-length mirror. After I finished nursing, my bosom headed south with some major and alarming sagging. No wonder Mark didn't seem too romantically interested in me! The sight made *me* want to gag! The fear of getting old became a major concern. I wasn't the young, firm thing I once was by any shot.

I soon realized motherhood would not fill the void in my heart either. My mood swings became even more dramatic. It wasn't much help that Amber was not a good sleeper. She never once slept through the night until she was a toddler. I became delirious at times from lack of sleep. Instead of using Amber's rare naps to catch up on sleep, I cleaned the house. Shortly after her birth, I suffered from an intense sinus infection that gave me the worst headaches I had ever experienced. Mark wasn't much help. The day after I came home from the hospital with Amber, he left for a month long training exercise. When he was able to squeeze in a brief phone call home, he didn't even ask about her. I finally mentioned Amber, and his blasé response was, "Oh, yeah, how is it?"

It?!

Let me just say, Mark's involvement with Amber's infancy was quite minimal. Despite the laundry list of things I was miserable with, I somehow didn't realize just how unhappy I truly was until my first trip home for my sister-in-law's Michigan wedding.

We had a wonderful visit with my husband's family that October, 1983. I arrived with a terrible case of bronchitis, but after seeing a doctor and getting some much needed rest thanks to my in-laws doting on Amber, I recovered quickly. Before long, it was time for me to head to Albany to see my Mom. Mark dropped me off and, due to his work schedule, hopped a flight back to Germany. I was to follow three weeks later after visiting my Gramma, who now spent her winters in Florida.

I was at Mom's for a few days in upstate New York, when she said a long-time family friend wanted to see Amber. Mom told me previously that Natalie had become a Christian. My first reaction was, "Listen, if she starts with this Jesus stuff, I'm going to feel really uncomfortable. My faith is just fine, thank you very much." My mother assured me that Natalie never bugged her about it, so I shouldn't worry.

Natalie was my mom's closest friend for years. She lived with her husband on what was once farmland, now converted into a beautiful homestead. Having an enormous amount of money and a hard work ethic, they had turned a huge barn into a magnificent home that could have been featured in any decorating magazine. Natalie's expertise in antiques, fine rugs, and overall decorating savvy made the converted barn into a magnificent showplace. They did it all with their own bare hands, too! This was a woman I had always admired for her moxie, generous nature, and big heart. She was there for me when I was growing up, especially after my parents' divorce. Instead of always staying home alone while my mom and Gramma worked, I had the option of spending time with her. She fed me fantastic meals or snacks, took me with her to run errands, and opened their home to me, making me a part of their family. Her children from another marriage were grown and lived elsewhere, yet she treated me like one of her own. She is a striking, dark-haired, tall, attractive woman originally from Georgia. Natalie has a stubborn no-nonsense nature, and when she wants something, it's best to move out of her way!

As I drove up to the house, warm memories tumbled through my mind. One enjoyable experience after another literally flashed before my eyes. I parked in the driveway, took my Amber from her car seat, and walked up to the house ready to show her off. Natalie greeted me with a huge hug and a hearty welcome. As I walked over that familiar threshold, I had no idea I was heading towards certain events that would change my life forever.

Chapter 5

The Biblical Elite

No statement to many Christians could be more emotionally charged than that of, "Jesus Christ is not God." I can understand this. I was reared in a Christian denomination that taught the Godhead as a trinity.

—Wierwille, *Jesus Christ is Not God*

* * * * *

I sat in Natalie's ornate living room, visiting with her and experiencing the same happiness I always had when in her home. The barn's original beams, dark, exposed, and unfinished, ran across the ceiling. Natalie's years as a prosperous antiques dealer found them cluttered with everything from dried floral arrangements to antique farm equipment. Antique oriental rugs dripped from the walls onto the floors, their deep hues of tan and burgundy seeping into every aspect of the room. The overcast day allowed Natalie the use of her many Tiffany lamps to provide most of the lighting, casting a soft, subtle glow.

As Natalie hovered over Amber, I truly could see a change in her. She was tranquil, and far less abrasive. We chatted a bit, then finally settled in the family room, which had better lighting. One thing I had always observed about Natalie was that despite all of her money (which I thought at the time to be the answer to everything), she wasn't content. Sometimes, her unhappiness would surface in frequent displays of temper, yet the woman sitting across from me that day was at peace.

Attempting to form my thoughts into words, she cut me off in classic Natalie style by saying, "You want to know why I'm not such a witch anymore, right?" I told her I wouldn't have worded it quite like that, but yes! What had caused this change? She told me, "God."

Natalie reached over to a nearby table for her Bible to quote some Scripture. To my amazement, I noticed that the pages were worn, and numerous notes and highlighting covered almost every page. She actually was *into* this God stuff! She seemed so genuinely happy! Suddenly, as if the proverbial floodgates were opened, questions started pouring from my lips. These were serious *life* questions. Living near what was then the East German communist border, I had deep concerns about nuclear war—or any war for that matter. I had to fly back to Würzburg in two weeks, as well as a quick flight to Florida, and was terrified of boarding the plane. Natalie gave me answers to my fears by reading directly from the Bible, and impressing me with knowing just where to turn for these answers. She said that if I were "born again of the Spirit," then it wouldn't matter what war happened—God was in control—and if I were "saved," I'd go to heaven despite what happened here on earth. Regarding my fear of flying, she said death was of Satan, and if I believed strongly enough, God would land the plane safely. God protected his children and had complete power over Satan.[2]

My eyes must have widened to saucers. She wasn't quoting some minister's interpretation from the Bible; she was reading directly from it and it all made sense!

She told me that a course taught by Dr. Victor Paul Wierwille was the key to opening the door to the happiness life had to offer. It's what happened to her, and as I could see, she was a deeply happy woman. She also told me that Ronald Reagan himself was a believer (only Wayers are "true" believers), and that "the Doctor" had recently visited him for a personal meeting in Washington, D.C. (This visit and Reagan's involvement in TWI was total Way folklore.) I was absorbing it all like a sponge. She told me how the class called Power for Abundant Living (PFAL for short) taught her how to read the King James Version of the Bible (the only translation that Way believers use; Wierwille claims it to be the closest translation to the original text). She proclaimed that she was now a Born Again Christian, saved, and certain of going to heaven.

As I sat listening, I realized immediately that I wanted to be a part of this and take that class as soon as possible. I had never met anyone who seemed so certain they wouldn't go to

---

[2]Most teachings from The Way were biblically accurate or so close—like the ones mentioned here—that distinction between false teachings and the actual meaning our Lord intended became a struggle once I left the cult. I had to read the Bible again as if learning it for the first time. The inaccuracies were slight in some cases; it is only with God's help and a wonderful Bible called *The Life Application Bible* with its extensive notes that I was able to sort the garbage from the truth.

hell. That *alone* was a reason to buy into this whole thing! I was quite hooked—right there, that very hour!

In the subsequent days following my visit with Natalie, we talked almost daily by phone. She encouraged me to get a King James Version of the Bible, which I promptly did. She said that she was able to find a place in Germany where I could take the class once I got back home.

The time came for me to fly to my Gramma's house in Florida for a visit before returning to Germany. I was able to board the plane with only a vestige of the fear I had when coming to the States. I believed God would keep the plane aloft, and I landed safely in Tampa to prove it!

While I was in Florida, Natalie arranged for me to visit a Way meeting called a "Twig." The local Bible study groups were called this because The Way believes that like a tree, the life of the ministry is in the Twig, where the Leaves (believers) gather. The "accuracy" of God's Word is taught in the home, just as it was in the first century church. Weirwille claims, "The early Church, the Body, as recorded in the book of Acts and the Church Epistles, developed a pattern for its growth in various localities…small supervised meetings, called churches, were held in private homes with a head elder or pastor overseeing each home unit."[3]

At my first meeting, I didn't feel quite right even though the people were nice. I wasn't able to put my finger on why, so I chalked it up to my own personal limitations, and seated myself on the far side of the room, watching other people

---

[3] Wierwille, The New Dynamic Church: Studies in Abundant Living. American Christian Press. 1971 P.146

arrive. Everyone seemed to know each other, making me feel like the odd man out. I sat silently, waiting for someone to extend their hand and welcome me. Nothing.

The Twig leader opened with a prayer exactly on time. I was introduced and my welcome was met with a lackluster response. I didn't expect fanfare, but the less-than-enthusiastic reaction made me second-guess my desire to join this exclusive group.

We sang some songs from a book called *Sing along The Way*, a publication by TWI's own publishing company, American Christian Press. These song books were mostly original Way songs, but there were a few traditional Christian songs as well. I did not know any of the songs we sang that evening.

I was beginning to feel completely alienated when the Twig leader suddenly announced we would be hearing directly from God. He then called on someone by name and told him to speak in tongues and interpret. This fluid, foreign tongue filled the room, followed by its English interpretation. It was in the first person, as if God were speaking, and I recall it being something like, "My children, you are my precious children and I am the Lord your God. Keep my Word, hold it fast, taking a stand on the promises I have made to you..." blah, blah, blah. I was spellbound. The Twig leader then called on another believer to speak in tongues and the same thing would happen. I noticed each person had his or her own distinct foreign tongue; nothing sounded forced or fake. A third person was called on to give a word of prophecy. This person did not speak in tongues, but instead delivered the message in plain English. After a few more people were called on to provide us with prophetic words, the Twig leader said it was time to begin our lesson in the Word.

For two hours, I absorbed every aspect of their ritual. I was so stunned by the speaking in tongues, I cannot recall what was taught that night. I used my new KJV Bible, trying to follow along, but instead found myself reeling from the events I had just witnessed. This group also verified what Natalie had said about Ronald Reagan. They asked if I had ever seen him going to a church service. I had to admit, I had not witnessed our president ever going to church. They told me it was because he met with believers in a private setting, just like a Twig. Of course, all of this was a bunch of bologna, but at the time, I had no reason to doubt a family friend or these nice people, so I believed every word. The idea that Ronald Reagan was a believer, and that if I became a member of The Way I would be a part of "the biblical elite" just made me more fired up than ever. By the end of the night, my initial doubts were obscured by the charismatic activity, and I knew for certain I'd be taking that course once back in Germany.

When I did arrive in Würzburg, I began reading my Bible for hours every day. Occasionally, Natalie called to make certain I was still "on the right track," and to give me information regarding "the Class," as Wayers call it. It was to take place in Fulda, and the first session was scheduled for early April. In the meantime, I read the KJV Bible, its wonders unfolding before me.

As demonstrated in the Florida Twig meeting, I figured out The Way places a huge emphasis on speaking in tongues. This is supposedly proof positive that one is saved and "born again of God's Spirit" according to Way teachings. I didn't want to wait for the Class before I spoke in tongues. I was assured I would be taught how during the sessions, but I wanted to speak in tongues *yesterday*! Natalie refused to give me any concrete information concerning how to go about this, encouraging me to wait for the Class. Unable to accept this, I tracked down some believers in Germany and started asking questions. I was obsessed, and wanted detailed information.

I tracked down and called the couple hosting the Class. Tim and Cindy, an army sergeant and his wife, also encouraged me to wait until the Class. They were nice, but seemed a bit annoyed that I was rushing things. The second call I made that night was to a civilian living in Germany who had already taken the Class. He was kind and helpful. He told me that God gives the utterance, but that we must move our tongues and mouths ourselves to make the sounds (this is exactly the method that is used in the Class). God would take care of the rest. He suggested something that worked for him: just start talking gibberish out loud, as if making baby talk, and perhaps this could lead me to speaking in tongues as it had for him.

That very night, after Mark had gone to sleep, I sat in the little hallway bathroom of our tiny government quarters now in Schweinfurt, Germany. With the door closed, I attempted to apply what I had been told to do. I read a scripture passage The Way heavily emphasizes out loud:

That if thou shalt confess with thy mouth the Lord Jesus, and shalt believe in thine heart that God hath raised him from the dead, thou shalt be saved. For with the heart man believeth unto righteousness; and with the mouth confession is made unto salvation.[4]

With tears streaming down my face, I called out to God in prayer to show me "tongues." I begged God to give me this

---

4 Romans 10:9-10, KJV

miracle so that I would "know like I know like I know" (a familiar, routine quote from Wierwille), that I was saved. I was told that once I spoke in tongues, I would absolutely know that I would have eternal life and be lifted with Jesus when he came again to judge the earth. I then started speaking gibberish out loud. Within a few seconds, I was speaking in tongues rapidly and as fluently, as if it were my native language.

The joy I experienced at that moment is indescribable. There simply are no words to express the incredible, exhilarating emotion rushing through my entire being. I felt as if I could fly around the apartment. God was REAL! *I WAS SAVED!* I had *physical* proof of my salvation! The Bible was UNDERSTANDABLE! In his Word, God said this would happen, and *IT DID!*

It was well past midnight, but I ran into the bedroom and woke up Mark to tell him. Half asleep, he seemed quite unimpressed as I demonstrated my newfound ability. Not disheartened, I let him go back to sleep. Nothing was going to dampen the utter thrill of it all for me. Nothing! I locked myself in the hall bathroom with my Bible, and spoke in tongues for hours, crying and reading until dawn. Finally, I fell into bed exhausted, but very fulfilled.

I spoke in tongues for my private prayer—what Wayers use it for—every day, every chance I got. We were told that because we ourselves couldn't understand what we were saying, this was "perfect prayer" that Satan couldn't interrupt. Pure prayer was between the believer and God and I definitely wanted to purely pray as much as was humanly possible. I was fairly bursting with this new joy in my life, and the assurance that I was a Born Again Christian. I couldn't wait to take the Class! Although I would never have admitted it to myself at the time, that night, I found a new god in my life. It was The Way International and its founder, Victor Paul Wierwille.

Chapter 6

Guarded Enthusiasm

This is a book containing Biblical keys. The contents herein do not teach the Scriptures from Genesis 1:1 to Revelation 22:21; rather it is designed to set before the reader the basic keys in the Word of God so that Genesis to Revelation will unfold and so that the abundant life which Jesus Christ came to make available will become evident to those who want to appropriate God's abundance to their lives.

—Wierwille, *Power for Abundant Living*

* * * * *

As the days progressed, I continued reading my Bible faithfully. Natalie told me to stick to the New Testament, because this was addressed to the grace period church or Born Again believers of today. Revelation was also to be ignored because it wasn't addressed to us. The same reasoning was given for not concentrating on the Old Testament. I was told that although the whole Bible was given to us by inspiration of God, there were only certain portions we should study daily.

The PFAL Class fee had to be paid in advance and was nonrefundable should something have come up. While some families thought nothing of the forty dollars to cover the cost of our materials, it was a lot of money to us. I went about my life, sometimes sharing my new feelings about God with friends or neighbors. Something deep inside, however, held me back from revealing the group that I believed responsible for the new me. As the time to take the Class drew near, my husband cautioned me about getting involved in a religious group we had never heard of or knew nothing about. I instantly bristled, and chalked up his attitude to a lack of meekness before God. Yet despite myself, doubt crept ever so slowly into my mind.

The night before taking the Class, I went before the Lord in prayer, asking him to stop me if I was getting involved in a cult. The next morning, I still felt a lingering doubt about these intensive sessions. Despite my trepidations, I drove the hour and a half it took to get to Fulda—a city in northern Germany—where I would embark on the first leg of my spiritual journey.

I was warned by Tim and Cindy not to be late. Feeling like I had already annoyed them a bit, I really wanted to make a good impression by being punctual. I eased onto the Autobahn, and put the pedal to the metal trying to get to their government quarters on time. Midway through the trip, the car shifted dangerously to the right and I had great difficulty keeping the car under control. My heart sank. I had a flat. I would be late if I even made it at all. Having had flat tires before, I knew what to do. I instantly took my foot off of the accelerator and slowed down, trying to get safely off the road. At the same time, I began to speak in tongues, totally panicking that I would be late for my very first PFAL class. I called out to God, asking him to prevent me from being late. There were no other cars around me that early morning, so I am the only witness to what happened next. It will sound impossible, but it happened this way.

The car righted itself.

Feeling the change, I pressed gingerly on the accelerator, and the car smoothly gained speed as the shock set in. It couldn't be! I didn't have a flat anymore! GOD HAD FIXED MY FLAT! Having experienced flat tires before, I knew what they felt like. At that moment, it was as if my doubts dissolved and my brain hoisted a flag boldly declaring, "THE WAY IS THE ONLY WAY." Assurance that I was doing the right thing by taking the Class came over me, and I knew with certainty that God had intervened, righting my crippled car, because he wanted me to take that class. God was going to show me his true Word through TWI.

I remember entering Tim and Cindy's house right on time. Meeting Tim face to face, I envied Cindy for having a husband so devoted to God. Never a terribly shy person, even in new group situations, one of the first things I did was share the miracle of my flat tire's recovery. My tale was met with guarded enthusiasm. I had expected more of a reaction, but was too excited to be disillusioned. The Florida Twig had been less than exuberant as well, and had I not had that experience already, this indifference may have dampened my mood. Instead, I joyfully joined the others, eager and ready to begin.

There were about fifteen people total taking the Class. Before this first session, we had been given a huge white

binder filled with notes and charts, along with two books—
Power for Abundant Living and *Receiving the Holy Spirit
Today*—both written by Wierwille. We were told not to take
notes or even ask questions at any time during the sessions.
These weekend sessions would be from 9:30 in the morning
until 5:00 in the evening, with only a single, one-hour break
for lunch. Normally, the Class was held during weekday
evenings, but due to some military members in our group, an
exception had been made to accommodate their erratic hours.
At the end of the entire three-weekend session, if we still had
questions, we would be allowed to ask them. We were told to
watch the videotapes closely, and they would answer most of
the questions we had. When all of the "alumni" present talked
about Wierwille, it was done in hushed, reverent tones as if he
were Christ in the flesh. He was almost always referred to by
his one-word title, "Doctor." The entire atmosphere was
oppressive and the fear of disapproval was subtly instilled.
Yet I was hungry to begin, so I overlooked my uneasiness.
After a brief prayer by our host, we embarked on our first
mind-control tape.

Chapter 7

The Class

He [God] spoke to me audibly, just like I am talking to you now. He said He would teach me the Word as it had not been known since the first century, if I would teach it to others.
—Wierwille, quoted in Whiteside, *The Way: Living in Love*

* * * * *

The very first session lasted approximately seven hours. We had exactly one hour, and *only* one, to use the bathroom, eat lunch, or relax. We were *strongly* encouraged not to leave the room at any time. It was reiterated that the reason for not taking notes was due to the fact that, while writing, we could miss a key word or concept taught. The alumni encouraged us by telling us we would be surprised how much the mind could absorb just by listening carefully. This made me slightly uneasy. However, the explanation that we could have the privileged opportunity of viewing the tapes again at no further cost at any subsequent PFAL teaching diminished my doubts at the time. It all explained the presence of the alumni gathered. I reviewed the rules in my head: no note taking, no reading ahead in any of the materials given us, and definitely no questions until we "graduated." I could see now why my probing questions on speaking in tongues had been met with disapproval.

Almost from the very first moment Wierwille began talking, I was mesmerized. There was something about this "man of God" that held me, as well as the others in the room, spellbound. When he began to tell me about the Bible, I simply became euphoric. It was as if a huge door had been opened. Behind the door was KNOWLEDGE! I could have knowledge AND be saved! It just doesn't get any better! It is so difficult to describe the thrill I experienced with each passing hour. I was practically hyperventilating. In fact, I knew very little about TWI before that fateful day when I watched my first tape of "Doctor" teaching things I had never been told about the Bible. The more I listened, the more I was in awe. The problem was, he mixed truth with lies. As I absorbed the tapes like a frenzied woman, I had no idea how to recognize those lies, because I had no biblical knowledge to base it on. Despite that spark of skepticism that was somewhere deep inside, I believed Dr. Wierwille, and became a true, devoted Wayer.

During that first day of video lecture, I was bombarded with biblical "truths" as revealed by Wierwille. He was raised in a Fundamentalist atmosphere, and when he graduated from high school, he attended Mission House College and Seminary in Plymouth, Wisconsin, and in 1940 graduated with a bachelor of divinity degree.[5] The back cover flap of the PFAL book reads: "Dr. Wierwille's academic career includes Bachelor of Arts and Bachelor of Theology degrees from Mission House (Lakeland) College and Seminary, graduate studies at the University of Chicago and at Princeton Theological Seminary, where he earned the Master of Theology degree in Practical Theology. Later he completed his work for the Doctor of Theology degree." What is not mentioned is that this Th.D. was actually garnered from Pike's Peak Bible Seminary in Manitou Springs, Colorado. Yet *Christianity Today* reported in an article titled "A Degree from Pike's Peak" that there is a question about the credentials of this institution.

"In a letter from the Colorado Commission on Higher Education, a state official says that Pike's Peak seminary had no resident instruction, no published list of faculty, and no accreditation, and no agency of government supervised it. It offered its degree programs by 'extramural' methods, involving the sending of book reviews and papers by mail. The degrees, the official says, have no status except with the institution that conferred them."[6]

Wierwille claimed to have audibly heard from God concerning an interpretation of the Bible that had never been shown to anyone before. Thus, it is alleged Wierwille literally burned all the books in his library (the numbers vary from one thousand to three thousand), and started writing his own teaching library. He then embarked on creating a "Teaching and Research Ministry," proud to declare that it was *not* a

---

[5] Dictionary of Cults, Sects, Religions and the Occult/Mather/Nichols/pg. 308.
[6] Dictionary of Cults, Sects, Religions and the Occult pp.308-309.

church, but a "teaching ministry", as he spread the gospel of Victor Paul Wierwille.

Despite my captivation, there were still some conflicting emotions. A small part of me could see tiny red flags desperately signaling that something was not quite right. In fact, a rather large red flag popped up during the middle of that first session. I distinctly remember Doctor teaching about the fall of humankind. He said that it was *entirely* Eve's fault because she sexually seduced Adam (Wierwille really says this) and that is why Adam ate from the fruit of the forbidden tree. The fall of humankind was exclusively Eve's fault. Unfortunately, or in retrospect fortunately, I am not one to keep my mouth totally shut. I'm not a feminist, but recognized the unfairness of this charge. I decided to speak up, and did so while they were changing the tapes. I made my point in my typical less-than-serious manner.

"Seems to me Adam could have said no. I mean, when she offered him that apple, it's not as if he hadn't been told not to eat it...I don't care how titillating her nightgown was!"

There was an instant air of disapproval from the Twig leaders Tim and Cindy, and the alumni present. The rest of the class laughed. I felt uneasy, but went on.

"Seriously! He could have just as easily said no as Eve could have. And *she* hadn't had the *direct* order from God as Adam did. After all, God told Adam about the tree of knowledge *before* he made Eve. Seems to me she only heard the news secondhand, so shouldn't Adam shoulder more of the responsibility?"

I trailed off, feeling especially uncomfortable as I began noticing the very obvious and intense glares of disapproval from the Twig leaders. I remained silent until the lunch break.

During the welcomed reprise from the intensive teachings, we went to another room where food had been provided for us. It wasn't anything fancy, but our hostess had obviously gone to some trouble preparing many nice dishes. Talk almost immediately turned to the point I had brought up, and a lively discussion followed. I noticed how quickly both Cindy and Tim managed to interrupt the conversation and turn the subject to something else. I thought it quite peculiar—this preoccupation with our harmless opinions—but brushed it off as we returned to the living room for more of Doctor.

After class, I drove the hour and a half home. I dropped into bed, drained yet exhilarated. Within minutes, I received a call from Cindy. She said she had talked with Reverend Werner Schmidt and his wife, Harriet, from Der Weg (German for The Way) in Bonn, Germany. I could sense Cindy's uneasiness relating this to me. Harriet apparently felt my outburst was completely unacceptable and such insubordination had to stop immediately.

I was crushed. I couldn't understand why we couldn't just talk. What was wrong with that? I knew we couldn't ask questions, but I wasn't asking anything, I was just commenting. Cindy told me that when she related to Harriet what I had said, Harriet claimed Satan himself must have put those words in my mouth. The fact that I had even *attempted* to contradict Doctor, regardless of the lighthearted manner, was a horrible breach of some kind of ethics. Deep down, something inside me wanted to blurt, "Hey, we're not talking about Jesus Christ; he's just some preacher man!" Instead, I muttered something about being very sorry.

As extreme as the high was from that first day, the low was equally as fierce. I stood frozen, holding the phone, mouth agape, as Cindy told me I would be forbidden from finishing the Class unless I promised not to cause trouble again. Tears stung my eyes, but I didn't want her to know this. I agreed to be careful about commenting, and we awkwardly said our good-byes.

Me? Possessed by a demon? I was both frightened and ashamed all at the same time. These were people that I believed to have *total, absolute* knowledge of the Bible, and the things of God. They were the experts; they must be right! That first night, I didn't get much sleep. The next day, Sunday, I was uncharacteristically quiet even during the one-hour break. I also noticed, much to my broken heart, that the rest of the members of the class were distant to me. I eventually took Cindy aside and asked how to get rid of this unwanted demon she told me I had. She told me to be obedient, and to pray that I wouldn't have a spirit of rebellion about me. She assured me I did "just fine" that day, to continue praying, and not to worry. Easy for her to say! I somehow managed to finish the rest of the sessions without incident.

Upon "graduation," we received a small but impressive looking "diploma." In the very last part of the Class, the new recruits are expected to speak in tongues. The Way believes it to be the *only* concrete proof of a person's salvation. This ability is demonstrated in front of everyone upon demand. If by some fluke one isn't able to "manifest," then the person is taken into a room alone with one of the Twig leaders or alumni present and "led" into speaking in tongues. Great emphasis is placed on this happening. After about ninety minutes, everyone "manifested" and we were official graduates. I clearly remember feeling relief that I had already been speaking in tongues because the pressure would have made me sweat. At the same time, this supernatural occurrence just made me that much more certain that The Way was the *only* way! There was something absolutely fascinating about a room full of people, previously unable to speak in tongues, after watching hours of lecture by Wierwille suddenly start speaking in these odd languages. The expression on those who spoke was priceless. This occurrence was another reason that deepened my belief in what Wierwille taught. How could this *not* be from God?! Witnessing this with my own eyes and ears made it all somehow real, and left absolutely no doubt in my mind that I was a part of something that had come directly from God. A tangible, physical proof that we were now *officially*, brand new, saved, Born Again Christians!

Although I behaved myself until the last day, I remained an outsider. I was never able to click with these people after that first session, and this hurt me deeply. I tried telling myself it didn't matter, but it did. This was the family of God, and I could not find my place. Despite my happiness at completing the course, there was also sadness. I regretted I had caused problems and alienated myself from my classmates because of my big mouth. I felt both guilt and condemnation. Over the course of my six-year involvement with this group, I continually felt as if I just weren't measuring up. It nearly broke my spirit in two.

Although I wanted desperately to fit in, try as I might, I still opened my mouth when I observed inconsistencies or contradictions. The first class may have been my first experience making waves, but it definitely was not to be my last.

Chapter 8

Growing in the Word

"The Word of God is the will of God."

—Wierwille

* * * * *

The entire PFAL session lasted approximately thirty-three hours. What I know now, but did not know then, was that I was slowly and systematically brainwashed. In her article, "Mind Control: The Way of The Way," Lorraine Ahern states:

> In a definitive mental health study of "totalist" groups for Harvard University, Robert Jay Lifton identified eight steps to mind control used by Communist Chinese in the 1940s. Psychologists claim that former Way members describe identical methods.

The Wrong Way

"Without question," echoes an Ohio psychologist who in seven years has counseled about 50 members leaving The Way; "all those people have been able to identify every point, not just in a mediocre situation but in a very definite way." Psychologists say the tedium of The Way's video course amounts to "information overload." It is a state of mild hypnosis which psychologists Flo Conway and Jim Swigelman...say results from overloading the sensory nerves.[7]

Having exposed myself to hour after hour of videotape lecture, I was subtly fed the lies of Satan himself. It wasn't just a man I heard them from, but the very powers of darkness teaching through those tapes. Today, I can read the very same verses I read over and over during the six years I was in the cult, and many mean something totally different than they did to me then. The scales were in front of my eyes, and I believed only the lies of this mind-numbing cult. To the outside world, I lived my daily life as any normal mother and wife, yet I had been brainwashed.

There are two prominent misconceptions about people who have been brainwashed. The first is that the person walks around as if in a Hollywood B movie, zombielike and unable to function in a normal fashion. The other misconception is that merely because the person says they are not brainwashed, then it must mean they are not. This simply is not so. There are many cults today with members who are completely

---

[7]Lorraine Ahern, "Mind Control: The Way of The Way," *The Capital*, 2 April 1986, front page.

brainwashed—believing bizarre things, yet leading a productive, normal existence to those who only see the surface of their lives. Noted psychologist and professor, Dr. Margaret Singer, chronicles in her book, *Cults in Our Midst*, how thought reform works:

> *Brainwashing is not experienced as a fever or a pain might be; it is an invisible social adaptation. When you are the subject of it, you are not aware of the intent of the influence processes that are going on, and especially, you are not aware of the changes taking place within you.*
>
> *In his memoirs, Cardinal Mindszenty wrote, "Without knowing what had happened to me, I had become a different person." And when asked about being brainwashed, Patty Hearst said, "The strangest part of all this, however, as the SLA delighted in informing me later, was that they themselves were surprised at how docile and trusting I had become....It was also true, I must admit, that the thought of escaping from them later simply never entered my mind. I had become convinced that there was no possibility of escape....I suppose I could have walked out of the apartment and away from it all, but I didn't. It simply never occurred to me."*
>
> *A thought-reform program is not a one-shot event but a gradual process of breaking down and transformation. It can be likened to gaining weight, a few ounces, a half pound, a*

> *pound at a time. Before long, without even noticing the initial changes—we are confronted with a new physique. So, too with brainwashing. A twist here, a tweak there—and there it is: a new psychic attitude, a new mental outlook....[8]*

After taking the first brainwashing session, I began attending the Twig meetings in Fulda once a week, usually on Sunday mornings, although they were available Wednesdays as well. The long drive started taking its toll. I was hounded to attend more often but just couldn't, and the resulting guilt was an ever-nagging presence. I hoped each Twig session would bring me to a better relationship with the members; however, I still remained a distant participant in the weekly home Bible meetings. There was even a barbecue I was conveniently left out of. When I discovered it had taken place, I asked Tim and Cindy why I had been left out. They made noises as if they thought they had told me. It was obvious these "perfect" Christians were not telling the truth. I felt deeply wounded.

My husband remained a steadfast skeptic, beginning a wedge between us. Despite the obvious lack of warmth extended by the local Twig leaders, my heart was on fire for God's Word and I never missed a day of reading, followed by prayer. I was a sponge. Mark's lack of enthusiasm began to eat at me. I wanted to become the "right" kind of Christian quickly so that, perhaps, by my example, Mark would become interested. I really tried to conform.

---

[8] Margaret T. Singer and Janja Lalich, *Cults in Our Midst: The Hidden Menace in Our Everyday Lives*, reprint ed. (San Francisco: Jossey-Bass), 61-62

One big Way rule is that all symbols of the cross are to be rejected. The persistent claim throughout my time in the group was, "If Jesus had died from a gunshot wound, would you wear a gun around your neck?" I am ashamed to admit I not only repeated this Way logic, but also gave away the cross a beloved family member had given my first daughter in honor of her birth. I deeply regret doing so to this day. I truly considered it a pagan symbol at the time, and my ambition to become one of God's elite superseded all else...including my common sense.

The Way considers itself a "teaching ministry," not a religion. All religions and denominations are looked upon with great disdain. Jews were demon-possessed and maligned. Catholics were openly and frequently scoffed at. Because of my experiences with the Catholic church, it was easy to ridicule it even though I was raised Roman Catholic. We were told that the more we learned about God's Word (only through The Way of course), the more we would know as compared to the rest of the world's religions. The feeling of exclusivity prevailed. The leaders, while claiming to possess no more or less Holy Spirit than any other believer, were nonetheless treated like royalty (and more or less expected such treatment). The leaders were almost always men. The Way believers were far "superior" because they had received the knowledge directly from Doctor, who had heard audibly from God. Wierwille believed he was given the only truth God had shown anyone since the first century church. The Doctor was, in essence, a modern day prophet although he was never referred to as this. He was "chosen," handpicked by God, to tell the world about the mistakes all other Christian organizations have made about the Bible since the first church. To follow this train of logic, Wayers are told they are the "chosen" believers. The snide arrogance that lies underneath the clean-cut facade of Wayers can easily surface when Way doctrine is challenged.

I wanted to know the most. I wanted to fill my mind with every piece of material that Doctor taught. This led me to take the Intermediate Class in June of 1984 at a cost of forty-five dollars. Again, we watched hour after hour of Doctor on video, culminating with a refresher course in speaking in tongues, but adding the ability to interpret. Admittedly, that last day was done in a very controlled and orderly fashion. Each of us was brought into this next phase carefully. When called upon, we were told to speak in tongues and then say the first words that came to our minds out loud. After several hours of this, I felt my interpretation wasn't as godly as the rest sounded, but I kept it to myself, secure in the knowledge (at least for the time being) that I had been exposed to many more hours of biblical wisdom than most people are taught in a lifetime. I believed there was simply no comparison because those other Christians weren't *really* Christians unless they had heard and believed what Doctor taught. Now, *saying* this to a Wayer will instantly make them defensive, as this would not be their thought process. Phrases like, "I don't believe any so-called doctrine," "I believe the truths of the Bible," and "Anyone who doesn't know these truths is ignorant of what God's Word really says," are responses any good Wayer would recite. They also say that they believe "no man," but in the same breath adhere to anything Doctor taught as if he were God himself. In reality, Wayers not only believe doctrine based on what one man teaches, but they also exalt him as a prophet. They are brainwashed into doing so.

Throughout this time and for the rest of the year, Natalie was in touch sporadically. Because I didn't quite fit in with the Fulda crowd, I depended more and more upon Natalie's counsel. I wrote at least once a week, and because she was a family friend, exchanged news and questions through my mother when we talked on the phone. My mom, an ex-Catholic-turned-atheist, merely passed along the information, happy that Natalie and I had renewed our close relationship of earlier days. Natalie never seemed too thrilled to answer my constant—and I mean *constant*—questions, but I had no one else to turn to. I wanted to know everything Doctor and TWI contained.

During that year, I also had an encounter with a Methodist minister that merely confirmed to me that TWI was far superior to what was being taught to the rest of the religious world. I can't recall the exact circumstance, but I happened to be on the phone with the minister one afternoon. He had a doctorate in theology and was quite full of himself. I had hour upon hour of elite Wierwille theology and was also quite full of myself, as I had been taught to be. Our conversation turned to what TWI refers to as "the nine manifestations of the Holy Spirit" found in 1 Corinthians 12:1-12 (1) word of wisdom, (2) word of knowledge, (3) faith, (4) gifts of healing, (5) the working of miracles, (6) prophecy, (7) discerning of spirits, (8) speaking in tongues, and (9) interpretation of tongues.[9]

Wayers were told that every Way believer could operate these "manifestations." We were not to use the word *gifts*. According to Wierwille, other denominations incorrectly taught that these were gifts. Wierwille said that the "accuracy of God's Word" reveals the gift was the holy spirit (lowercase because this holy spirit is different from God who is Holy

---

[9] 1Corinthians 12:1-12, KJV

Spirit), and that the nine manifestations were the operation of the gift (holy spirit.)

When I mentioned that I spoke in tongues (the minister apparently could not) he told me that speaking in tongues was for the apostles and not for modern-day Christians. There are differing opinions about this subject. As true Christians, we should not focus on what our differences are, but what it is that we agree on concerning a Christ-centered life of service to him. At that time, I was far too arrogant to let this man's comments go unchallenged, and felt that what I was taught was the truth and the *only* truth, period. I also felt *he* needed to know the truth, and I was going to be the one to tell him.

In my smuggest voice, I said, "Why, Pastor, that's not what the Bible tells us."

We proceeded to have a testy discussion. When a Wayer is challenged on biblical knowledge, they think they come from a vastly superior plane. To even *consider* challenging one who possesses this exceptional knowledge is a waste of time. People should just listen and be in awe of the elite Wayer's knowledge, and immediately sense the futility of disagreeing. This isn't something a member will readily admit, but they are the true feelings of almost any Way believer.

The more I talked with this minister, the more convinced I became that this man knew very little about God's Word. He knew far less than me, or so I was egotistical enough to conclude. To be quite frank, TWI drums *many* accurate Bible lessons into the eager recruit. I would venture a guess that at least 70 percent of these lessons are accurate. It is the remaining 30 percent that is the darkest, most twisted evil.

So there I was, leafing through my Bible, matching this man of the cloth verse for verse. The biggest turning point for me was when he boldly declared, "Why in the world do you place so much emphasis on the least important so-called manifestation?" I asked what he meant by "least important." He said that tongues was listed last in the Bible, therefore making it the least important. (Speaking in tongues is listed second to last in 1 Corinthians 12:10.) Doctor himself had taught that many Christian ministers make the mistake of calling tongues the least important manifestation. He predicted that they would often make the mistake of calling it the "last-listed gift," thus proving the ignorance of the average man of the cloth.

As insignificant as this may seem to the average person, it was *most* significant to me, especially since I was such a "babe" in TWI. To me, this was further proof that Wierwille had knowledge not given to the common man. The little details we learned were amazing "corrections" the enlightened Wierwille made concerning what the rest of the Christian world supposedly had not learned, weren't taught, or learned incorrectly from others who attempted to teach the Bible. (Another such teaching by Doctor is that FOUR men, not two as history has always portrayed, were crucified with Christ.) As corrupt as I know these teachings are now, they made *absolute*, logical sense to me when I learned them. Until I was delivered from the spiritual, vise-like grip this cult had on me, I believed in the lessons as surely as I had ever believed anything to date in my life. I was spiritually blinded.

So there I was, just some new Way believer, and yet I knew more than a Methodist minister, twice my age, who had been studying the Bible longer than I had been alive! This experience just proved Doctor right! There was no doubt in my mind that Wierwille was truly a prophet of God!

I took this as an unadulterated, no-doubt-about-it sign that I had obtained vastly superior biblical knowledge through

Victor Paul Wierwille. This was a crucial turning point for me. I believed there would be no turning back. I wanted all the way into The Way!

While "growing in the Word"[10] and Wierwille doctrine, I gave birth to my second daughter, Allison, in November of 1984. That December, we left Germany for a tour in the States. Next stop, Los Angeles, California. I had high hopes that when I found a Twig there (I was told in advance that they were all over California), I would finally find a Way family that would accept me and make me feel at home. I never dreamed this would be the beginning of my falling out with the leadership in California, taking me all the way to the headquarters in New Knoxville, Ohio. This new phase would make my feelings of isolation and insecurity multiply as I became convinced I would never measure up to the expectations God had placed upon my stubborn little head.

---

[10] Wayspeak for studying the Bible and having spiritual growth as a result.

BOOK TWO

IN THE WAY

Chapter 9

The California Way

"In September of 1984, Dr. Victor Paul Wierwille made a single-sentence suggestion to Rev. L. Craig Martindale while they were flying home to The Way International Headquarters on *Ambassador One:*[11] 'Maybe you ought to think about putting a book together, son, made up of short statements I've spoken over the years which have blessed people.' That was the end of the subject. The two men, the Founding President and the President of The Way International never spoke of it again."[12]

---

[11] *Ambassador One* was the private jet Wierwille used to fly wherever he chose.

[12] *Life Lines – Quotations of Victor Paul Wierwille.* American Christian Press, New Knoxville, OH 1985, p ix.

The Wrong Way

* * * * *

We moved to Mission Hills, California, a pleasant city located in the San Fernando Valley. Mark became part of the Army Recruiting Battalion for Los Angeles, and immediately dove into his duties. We rented a nice, three-bedroom house in a neighborhood considered crime-free by L.A. standards. This meant there weren't any crack houses on the *immediate* corner, but it did not mean there was no crime. Amber remained an alert and active toddler, constantly probing. Allison was four months old and already sleeping through the night, much to my delight. She was a beautiful baby with a feisty spirit. A friend of mine, whose husband worked in advertising, told me Allison had "the look" and begged me to begin a portfolio. I just couldn't imagine putting my daughters through that. Plus, being an army family, we never knew where we would land the next day.

When we settled, the first thing I did was advertise for a sitter in the classifieds. Next, I contacted the people I was told would be my Twig leaders, Jim and Diane Ballard. I asked Mark to go with me to this first meeting and he agreed. We drove to their small but very charming condominium. Diane had decorated it beautifully. They were a newly married couple, without children, yet they welcomed Mark and me and our babies with open arms. I believed I had finally found my church family, and became convinced that these wonderful people would be the vehicle to bring Mark to a knowledge of the God The Way taught.

We began to go as a family to weekly fellowship meetings that were usually attended by no more than five to ten other people. Gone was the legalistic condemnation I had previously known from Way believers. Our Bible studies were warm, friendly gatherings. Although the Bible was taught, it was generalized readings from the Word instead of Wierwille and TWI dogma, usually preceded by prayer. We even sang from *Sing Along The Way.*

Due to Mark's ever pressing schedule, he was soon unable to attend meetings, so I went alone. Getting a babysitter once a week and going to Jim and Diane's house was a welcome break from the daily humdrum of motherhood. I immediately became very close to these sweet, loving people. Jim and Diane were always supportive, lending a sympathetic ear when Mark's long hours and numerous trips out of town became burdensome. I felt like a single parent most of the time. I had two very young children, which limited my time away from home. We didn't have much money either. After buying groceries, paying the rent, utilities, and other debts, there was just a bit of spare change left for pocket money.

When Mark wasn't out of town, he was rarely home before 9:00 P.M. and often too exhausted to even eat a meal with me. Sometimes, he would actually fall asleep at the dinner table while I chattered away, trying to cram a week's worth of talk into one short evening. Between our strained financial status and feeling like a single parent in a large, unwelcoming city, I swiftly became dependent on my new friends in The Way. They, of course, generously took me under their wing.

One evening, in the middle of our Twig meeting, the Ballards' phone rang. Diane answered it. Just by the tone of her voice, I knew something was terribly wrong. When she got off the phone, she announced that Dr. Wierwille had died. It was May 20, 1985. A solemn moment I did not react much to. I had never met him and although I had submitted to listening to hours upon hours of tapes of him teaching us "the pure Word," I merely regarded him for just what he was: a mortal man. I believed him to be a very knowledgeable and gifted man, but still just a man. I could tell that a significant event had taken place. The rest of the Twig meeting was devoted to praying for Doctor, who had "gone to sleep" as Wayers put it, and for his family. Although no one from the Way ever admitted it to me, I knew that most believed him to be a very special, *chosen* man of God. Consequently, this would explain my untiring devotion to what he taught despite the numerous errors I soon began finding within TWI and the doctrine of Dr. Victor Paul Wierwille.

* * * * *

Early the next year, The Way organized a nationwide contest. It was called "The Way International Music Challenge." The entire Limb, or state of California, would compete in the contest in L.A. The winner would compete against other state winners from around the country at "the Rock of Ages"—a Woodstock-like annual gathering of thousands of Wayers from around the world near the headquarters in Ohio. A grand champion would then be selected at this event. Jim and Diane told me that participation in the state contest would be an opportunity to meet many Way believers. I decided to ask one of my Twig members, Bill Anderson, to accompany me because he was a talented musician and songwriter. I chose a song written by other Way faithful and distributed by TWI. It was an upbeat, lively tune, and Bill and I practiced it almost daily for over two months to perfect it for the contest.

I called Natalie to tell her I was entering the contest and was surprised by her condemnation of the entire competition. She complained that Christians should not be competing against each other, but still wished me luck. Natalie's remarks surprised me, but I brushed it off as nothing more than Natalie speaking her mind, which she had always done.

This was the very first indication I had that all was not perfect in TWI paradise. I had never heard *anyone*, thus far, criticize the leadership for a single decision they made. I recall one example that caused some complaining from Wayers. The leadership decided that "by revelation," all video material should be in Beta format. This decision was made despite the fact that even then Beta was obviously going by the wayside. It was annoying, because in order to purchase videos from The Way bookstore, you had to own a Beta VCR. The leadership scoffed at even the friendly criticism and demanded unwavering loyalty from its members. Their claim was that they (the leadership) were led by direct revelation from God in this and *all* decisions, so members were not to question *any* final decision.

The more I read the Word in my daily study, the more I had a heart to sing for God. I was convinced that my voice was a gift to be used to witness to others. I wanted my performance in the contest to be perfect. I expressed hopes of someday performing at "the Rock of Ages." Everyone who had ever attended told me that I hadn't lived until I had gone to one of these events. This became my goal. I wanted to someday perform at "the Rock," as it was called, and I was willing to work very hard to achieve this crowning glory. I shared these feelings with Jim and Diane, and Jim merely said that I had to "prove myself" in the ministry by singing at "lower level" meetings first. He expressed that he hoped this contest would be the beginning of a Way music ministry for me.

I hoped so too, and believed that this was my calling from God.

* * * * *

Before the big contest, I had heard through other Way members in my Twig that one contestant, Joe Sanders, was considering a divorce. Way leaders were very much against this and were against his participation in the contest. The gossip—because that is essentially what is was—centered around the disbelief that *anyone* would go against the leadership, as Joe was, by entering the competition despite being advised not to and refusing to back out.

Everyone talked about the group Blastout. They were the clear favorites to win. The talented members were professional musicians in L.A., all devoted Wayers of course, and had performed in various Way-sponsored gatherings across the country. I truly had no real hopes of winning against such tremendous opposition, but I felt the exposure was the important element concerning my performance.

The big day arrived. Knowing TWI's strict rules about being on time, I made the dress rehearsal (the same day as the performance) with an hour to spare. I was the last participant allowed a sound check, so I sat in the huge, rented auditorium and watched the other acts warm up. I knew no one except Mark, who had taken time off from work to support me. Before my sound check, we walked around a bit, but eventually sat down because not a single person greeted us or showed any interest in us whatsoever. There were many people milling around, setting up, and if it weren't for a printed schedule of events I received prior to coming, I wouldn't have known when my sound check was. I truly felt like an outsider, just as I had in Fulda. Again, Mark openly expressed to me that these people were "a little weird," excluding the Ballards and the Andersons.

Bill arrived, just minutes before my sound check. I only sang three stanzas before being abruptly interrupted by someone on the loudspeaker announcing our Limb leader had arrived. Apparently, the Reverend David Shafer wanted to meet with all the participants. As I left the stage, I silently noted how other acts, especially Blastout, were allowed to go over their pieces as long as they had wanted. But I chalked this up to negative thinking and pushed it from my thoughts.

It was also announced that all contestants were to meet backstage with David Shafer in exactly ten minutes, dressed and ready to perform. I frantically grabbed my performance clothes and dashed to the ladies' room to change. As I was applying the last bit of makeup a few hurried minutes later, a young girl rushed in, completely out of breath and obviously late. Other participants must have known about the meeting in advance, because there wasn't anyone else besides the two of us in the bathroom. She explained that right after her sound check, her babysitter had called her back home with a problem concerning her toddler. I silently thanked God that I had no such problems that day and made some sympathetic sounds as I started for the door. I did *not* want to be late. I admit I was a bit taken aback by her negative attitude. This is a no-no in The Way. A Wayer must be *positive*. Our lives as Way believers should be perfect (mine wasn't, of course, but I didn't let on to other believers it wasn't). Perfect health, finances, joy, and peace were available to all Way believers. If this wasn't the status of your life, then you weren't "believing properly." All negativity was directly from Satan. We were to speak in positive platitudes and I had already adopted this method. My self-righteous attitude must have shown as I sped out the door to meet our beloved Limb leader. With barely a polite good-bye to the troubled mother, I left the ladies' room.

Chapter 10

Seed of Disenchantment

Jesus Christ is referred to as God's Son 68 times in the New Testament; not one place is there "God the Son." To say that "Son of God" means or equals "God the Son" totally negates the rules of language, leaving it utterly useless as a tool of communication.

—Wierwille, *Jesus Christ Is Not God*

* * * * *

I had to ask one of the technicians where the meeting was being held. I ran all the way through the auditorium and through a backstage door. Just as I entered the room, the meeting began.

I looked around. Most everyone seemed to be acquainted with each other. I knew no one. There had been visiting going on before I arrived, but it came to an immediate halt as our leader began to speak. I scooted to the inside, left-hand corner of the room. I noticed that not only was David Shafer in a fine, expensive suit, but so were the men with him, hovering around him like bodyguards. Reverend Shafer, I was told, was in charge of The Way of California. I believed it necessary to listen to every word this minister said. After all, he must be a *great* man of God to have made it so far in TWI leadership.

He hadn't been speaking to us more than a few minutes when, in through the same door I had used, came the young mother from the ladies' room. A hush came over the room, as Shafer abruptly stopped mid-sentence to glare at her. Apparently, they had previously met because he said her name before launching into what I considered a tirade of dramatic proportion…all because she was late.

Shafer chewed her out in fine military fashion: the army drill sergeant putting his subordinate in her place. He walked towards her with a vicious look on his face as she sank into the easy chair near me. He planted himself directly in front of her, his feet shoulder-width apart, hands on hips, hollering down on her hung head about the evils of being late.

The look of shock must have been apparent upon my face. This demeaning lecture in front of everyone because she was a few minutes late? He raved on and on about respect for God's Word and his dedicated servants (meaning himself I assume). He then bent down so that he could be on her level, even with her face, as he questioned her commitment to this contest, The Way International, and then God himself. She was left quivering and on the brink of tears before he even stopped for a breath.

When he had finished with her, he resumed his little pep talk. The face that had just been so horribly contorted with anger over wasted time now melted into one of brotherly love and "like-minded" worship. I became angry. How could a person, no less a supposedly ordained minister, treat *anyone* like that? The image of her sitting in that chair, slumped over, head hung in shame, burned itself into my memory. My anger mixed with feelings of relief and guilt. I was thankful that I was not the object of Shafer's wrath, yet felt guilty for not bending down to comfort her. I didn't dare move.

Reverend Shafer finished up, and our meeting came to an end with a sanctimonious prayer blessing the proceedings. His flamboyant style sounded like an audition for a televangelist. I was totally disgusted.

I am also deeply ashamed to say that as Shafer ceremoniously left the room, the others followed, each walking by the young mother in the chair, noses in the air, as if she had a case of the plague. I was one of those people, and regret that to this day.

* * * * *

The contest began with much fanfare. The contestants were allowed to watch the program from the audience, as long as they went backstage one act prior to their performance. When Joe Sanders, the man with marital problems, came on stage, the curtains opened to an elaborate set. He sang two selections he had written, bringing the house down. My husband and I were very impressed. Not only was his music inspirational, but also the words had a beautiful Christian theme and message. He gave a remarkably talented performance.

Bill sat with Mark and me as we watched the show. He complained that not everyone had been allowed to use the entire stage, including me. Bill was told that we had to sing in front of the curtain (others were allowed to use the whole stage behind the curtain), and this disturbed him a great deal. He believed we wouldn't have a fair chance at winning. He pointed out that one of the judges was our Branch (area) leader, Don Meckley. Don was a close friend to a few of the members of Blastout. Furthermore, the wife of the drummer was also a judge. Bill said that since Don and the Blastout drummer's wife could hardly be considered impartial, they should have disqualified themselves from being judges. He insisted that Joe Sanders didn't have a chance of winning because the leadership, including Don Meckley, disapproved of his resistance to listen to counsel.

Not allowing the experience backstage with David Shafer to dampen my mood, I honestly didn't give winning a second thought and told Bill so. It truly was an honor to sing for God for the first time in my life, and that was what was most important to me. I didn't feel it was my place to comment on Bill's other observations, so I didn't. I had to admit, his concerns were valid, although negative in tone. Bill wasn't satisfied with my answer, but didn't mention it again that night.

It was my turn, and the excitement within me reached a fever pitch. Although I almost always put my entire heart into each performance, I outdid myself this time. I sang as if there would be no tomorrow. Not only that, but my voice was right on, going neither sharp nor flat. Judging by the audience's reaction, they too were pleased. I was satisfied with my upbeat performance, and even felt I might have a shot at the coveted first place title! I went back in the audience, taking my seat and thanking Bill for being my accompaniment (I was being judged by my singing capabilities alone; Bill was just my backup). Mark, always my biggest support and greatest fan, raved about how terrific I looked and sounded up there. People around us gave enthusiastic comments, and I basked in this positive attention from Way believers, hoping it would be the beginning of a wider acceptance by them in general…as if a good singing voice could win the approval of Way leadership.

Blastout was the last to perform. The curtains opened to rousing Christian rock so loud the lyrics couldn't be understood. Bill said that their recordings had been widely sold throughout the ministry, and it was evident they were playing to a receptive crowd, despite the blare.

The winner was Blastout.

Mark and I thought the first place honors should have gone to Joe Sanders. There was no comparison. I decided that Don Meckley, our beloved Branch leader, and I would have a talk. Between Shafer's outburst and this nutty contest, someone needed to say *something*, and that someone was going to be me.

Chapter 11

Confrontation

If it said a virgin shall bring forth a son your Bible would fall to pieces.
—Wierwille, quoted in McDowell and Stewart, *Handbook of Today's Religions*

* * * * *

I made arrangements to speak to Don Meckley at his home the following week. I arrived promptly, and was led into the living room of their beautiful, rented home. I had briefly met Don and his wife, Cathy, when we had first moved in, as well as at a few Twig/Branch meetings in his home.

They had two small children, and their squeals filled their San Fernando Valley home. Cathy was sitting on the couch but stood and warmly greeted me as I entered the room. I was led to a chair opposite Cathy, and as I sat down, Reverend Meckley offered me something to drink. I declined, although I actually would have liked a drink. I was a bit nervous about this meeting, but they made me feel welcomed...initially.

I had prayed long and hard concerning what I was to say. Not wanting to do anything I shouldn't, I called Natalie to discuss what I wanted to relate to Reverend Meckley and how I should recount it. She told me the situations I described seemed like valid concerns, and that going to the local leadership about it was the right thing to do. I was very impressed by Don's soft-spoken style of teaching the Bible. I was also told he was musically talented and had made several recordings for TWI that had sold well. I looked up to this man, and believed that when I came to him with my concerns, he would be understanding and receptive. Oh, how wrong I was.

I began by describing what had happened backstage before the talent contest. I told Don and Cathy about the young mother running into the ladies' room, and what had happened with her babysitter. I shared David Shafer's disdainful treatment of her in front of all the participants when she arrived a few minutes late for the meeting. I ended my comments by noting that all the participants were volunteers, and that this should have been a fun event, not taken so seriously. I remember saying this next comment distinctly: I said that although she perhaps was wrong in coming late, David Shafer grossly overreacted. I described in detail the mean-spirited way in which he corrected her. I also noted that he had just gone on and on, and that this was excessive to say the least.

As I talked, I noticed Don becoming angry. At first I thought he was angry because of Shafer's improper actions (Don wasn't present in the room for Shafer's meeting that night). However, it became crystal clear that his mounting rage was directed specifically at me.

When I stopped speaking, he asked me through clenched teeth if I had finished. I said yes, as far as my complaint about Reverend Shafer was concerned. I then received my own tongue-lashing.

Don Meckley was not a large man. He stood about five-feet, three-inches and could not have weighed more than 135 pounds. He stood up and began pacing, barely able to contain his fury. He admonished me for *daring* to question this great man of God. What right did I have to doubt what this servant of the Lord felt was fair? He told me that I should be ashamed of myself for even thinking such things.

I was shocked that I was being targeted. Something inside of me stood firm, refusing to back down. I was right. More importantly, I knew Reverend Shafer's action and complete disregard for the young mother were wrong. I had no idea at the time how I knew I was right, for I devoutly believed in not questioning Way authority, mostly because I thought they possessed a superior biblical knowledge that far surpassed my understanding. But I knew that David Shafer had been verbally abusive and downright mean to that young woman. Despite a timid voice telling me to back down, I didn't.

I stayed calm—a miracle itself because I had always had a quick temper—and told him that no matter what Reverend Shafer believed was the right thing to do in that situation, he executed it in a nasty and unloving manner. Don became so furious that his wife put her arm on his. He promptly tossed it off and fled the room, fists clenched.

I looked at Cathy, a bit shell-shocked. She tried to smooth the situation by saying perhaps I had misunderstood Reverend Shafer's demeanor. I firmly replied that his loud and lengthy reprimand would have been easy for a hearing-impaired mute to understand. He had been rude and blatantly abusive. She looked down at her hands and sat on the couch quietly. I could see I would have no support from her.

After a short time, Don reentered the room, obviously still angry, but much calmer. He started quoting Scripture, telling me I must be submissive to the leadership or some such hogwash. I knew, for the very first time, that I was dealing with a group of less-than-perfect men of God. Prior to these two incidents, I believed anything out of a Way leader's mouth was a direct revelation from God.

I abruptly interrupted him as he continued to rant about my alleged shortcomings.

"I know very well that I am to respect Way leaders, yet when they are doing things contrary to God's Word, I am not to respect their sin."

Don Meckley is not a violent man but *had* he been, I think he would have gone for my throat. His face turned crimson as he clenched his teeth and tried to regain his composure. I didn't let him. I hit him with my other complaint. Why not? Go for broke!

"Also, I thought that the judging of the talent contest was done unfairly. If someone is related to or knows the contestants very well, then they should disqualify themselves from judging the competition."

He looked at me incredulously. "Are you accusing me of cheating?"

"Absolutely not," I replied. "However, being best friends with members of the winning group doesn't exactly make you an impartial judge."

He left the room again, presumably to collect himself, again, and I decided that this was my cue to leave. It was clear

Confrontation

I was getting nowhere with the Reverend Meckley. I thanked Cathy for allowing me to come, and left.

I drove home, shaken and close to tears, but not from being chewed out. To my surprise, this was not what bothered me. What *was* so upsetting was that this supposedly superior ministry and its leaders, whom I placed on gilded pedestals, obviously had feet of clay. This realization not only hurt my heart for reasons I didn't understand then, but it also frightened me. I did not doubt myself for the first time; I was certain that what Reverend Shafer did was wrong. Yet this new feeling of lost confidence, in the very people running this organization I believed had a direct line to God, confused and terrified me. In retrospect, I did the only thing I could do at the time: I went straight into denial.

I never mentioned this incident to Reverend Meckley again, and vowed I would drop the entire subject altogether. I sold out for the time being and put my blinders on, something I would do quite frequently for the next several years, I'm ashamed to say. I just could not accept that the same organization that had taught me so much about the Bible was filled with such incompetent leaders. They were human, they made mistakes—but *not* when it came to teaching the Bible. And wasn't that the important issue? It turned out that I was very, very deceived.

Chapter 12

WOW

According to the accurate Word of God, how many men were crucified with Jesus? Two malefactors plus two thieves makes four people. All the teaching that we have had saying Jesus was on the center cross with one culprit to the right and the other to the left is proven faulty. The reason we have believed this is that rather than reading The Word, we believed the paintings we have seen.

—Wierwille, *Power for Abundant Living*

* * * * *

It was winter of 1986, and the talent contest incident seemed well behind me. When I ran into Don Meckley at subsequent Twig or Branch meetings, he was a bit distant but still courteous, so I tried to focus on his abilities as a teacher of God's Word rather than our confrontation.

I had started singing with Bill on a recording he was pouring his money into. I sang background vocals, and having never been in a studio before, enjoyed both the practice and the experience of the recording sessions. I believed we had a professional product, and was quite proud of our efforts. Bill was a talented musician and composer. He wrote the words and music, and arranged every selection. I tried to encourage Natalie to invest in our project, but she gently refused. This was a bit confusing because I knew she gave enormous amounts of money to the ministry, but I respected her right to decline.

Also during this time, some WOWs had moved in only a few blocks away from us. I was asked by our Twig leader to make them feel welcome. WOWs are "Way over the World" recruits who have been trained by TWI. They take three courses: the "Foundational Course" (which is the same thing as the Class/Power for Abundant Living/PFAL), the "Intermediate Course," and the "Advanced Course." Upon graduating from this training, they are sent to a place anywhere in the world chosen by Way leadership, given a small amount for moving expenses, and expected to "put into practical application" the principles they were taught. Actually, a believer wasn't required to take all the courses except PFAL in order to go WOW, but most WOWs had. If you were hungry enough and didn't mind being uprooted, you were a candidate. Once relocated, they were to take a stand on God's Word, and "believe" for a job, income, a home, etc. "Believing equals receiving," according to TWI. If you weren't living the abundant life, then your believing was faulty.

I took the telephone number of the WOWs and figured it was my Christian duty to help them out in any means I could. I called Monica and Matt the next day.

WOW

Monica answered the phone and was as sweet and bubbly as could be. I asked if there was anything she needed. Without hesitation, she asked if she could borrow a few sweaters since it still hadn't quite warmed up as much as she had expected it to in L.A. The winters and springs sometimes turned a bit chilly, so it was my pleasure to loan sweaters and jackets to Monica and her daughter. I gave her directions and she said she'd walk over that day (they were "believing" for a car). When she arrived, I opened the door to a very cute, petite fellow New Yorker. She was so much like the folks back home; I felt we would get along just fine, and at first, that seemed the case.

I told her again she could use the sweaters for as long as she needed them, but to return them to me as soon as her things came from home. I loaned her *nice* clothing. The WOWs were of celebrity status within The Way International. They "boldly" chose to relocate for one year of service to God, and were always honored at the end of their year of service at the Rock of Ages. We were standing in the dining room when she asked if I had any more sweaters she could use. I hesitated, because I had put the box away, and actually did not want to part with the rest since they were my very best sweaters. Feeling duty bound, I told her to wait, I'd see. I thought I had made it clear I was not inviting her down the hall to my room, but before I knew it, she had walked in behind me through my bedroom door.

She stood there while I got the box down, and began helping herself to the items in the box, practically pushing me out of the way, despite the fact I had not yet given her permission to take any of these items. I was quite miffed as she pulled out her selections and asked if she could take five extra cotton pullovers. Momentarily spineless, I said yes.

Then she went over to my dresser, picked up my cologne, and said, "Gee, this smells nice…since it's such a tiny bottle, can I have it? We're really strapped for cash, and I'd love some perfume." I replied yes to this request as well. I repeated, especially with these new things, that this was a loan until her mom shipped their clothes. She assured me that they would be returned the minute her mom sent the boxes UPS. As she went out the front door, she also asked if we could spare any cash. I wrote her a check for a small amount. She let out a cheery thank you as she dashed down the front walk, carrying several of my favorite sweaters and a bottle of my cologne.

I closed the door after her, a bit bewildered. I was not thrilled at all about the entire encounter, and yet this feeling was mixed with guilt because I thought I was supposed to help these people. I didn't speak to anyone about it until Monica's requests for money and transportation became more frequent.

I decided to call Bill and Jim to discuss what I began to believe was Monica taking advantage of me. She called almost daily requesting I take her on this or that errand. Her requests for "monetary donations" were constant. I decided to seek some counsel concerning how far my obligation to Monica, WOW or not, extended. I had no idea how to handle this any longer.

Jim seemed to think I was being taken advantage of, as did Bill. Jim suggested that he ask Don Meckley what to do. I realize, judging from my past experience with Reverend Meckley, one would think a huge warning flag would have popped up. However, I felt bolstered by the support I received from Jim and Diane as well as Bill. I also thought this was such a clear-cut case of Monica using poor judgment, that

Don would certainly see my side of the situation. Wrong again!

A few days later, Jim called me and said that Don hadn't taken the news favorably. Remembering that Reverend Meckley had taken kindly to these two, I didn't find this surprising, now that I thought about it. During a few meetings at the Meckleys' house, I noticed Monica and her husband, Matt, treated Don like a god, and this seemed to suit Don quite well. I believed it best to call Don and present my side myself.

Not a good idea I soon found out. He was barely able to contain his impatience as he told me to take the situation and "apply the Word to it." What kind of an answer was that? I tried describing my first meeting with Monica, and then the subsequent requests for money or taxi service, but this did not seem to impress him in the least. He rattled off scripture and told me "giving equals receiving," blah, blah, blah. I insisted that her constant demand on my time and pocketbook was becoming a burden and that I wanted him to advise me on what to do (I was finally convinced, however, that this man was no more a man of God than my Yorkshire terrier was). He just kept calmly, yet tersely, giving me platitudes. I finally ended the discussion by asking if he would please intervene and talk to Monica and Matt, since he knew them so well. He didn't agree he would, but I soon noticed Monica was no longer a daily presence in my life.

My next encounter with Monica was at a "burning the chaff" party at the Meckleys' home. The doctrine that every good believer should go through their closets and clean out things we were holding onto, yet not using, was based on the principle that "giving equals receiving." This was an opportunity to give away these items to someone who might be able to use them. Also, some possessions become overly important and we must focus on the fact that because we are Christians, everything belongs to God, not us. We were invited to bring items that we no longer wanted, and display them in the Meckley home, garage sale style. If another believer wanted any item, then they were welcome to take it, free of charge. The idea was a good one, so I willingly participated. I was actually thrilled to bring a short raccoon coat that I never wore, and thought, even though the weather was warm at the time, this might bless someone who otherwise might not be able to afford it.

I entered the Meckleys' home with my raccoon coat, a few other articles of clothing, and some knickknacks. I brought them into the kitchen where a temporary clothesline was in place. I put my items on the line, and began milling around. Every room had giveaways in it. I walked into the laundry room, and much to my astonishment, all of my sweaters on "loan" to Monica were hanging right in a row on a makeshift clothing rack. I couldn't believe it!

I ran to Cathy and whispered my discovery in her ear, asking if I could take my sweaters back. Although the atmosphere was a help-yourself type of gathering, I didn't want anyone to misunderstand and think I was being greedy by scooping up numerous sweaters. She decided to consult Don. The three of us stood around as I awkwardly explained Monica could not have misconstrued my intentions when she borrowed my clothes. He gave me a look of complete disgust. I realized that I sounded as if I were gossiping, so I stopped that line of discussion and asked if I could retrieve my property. He escorted me back to the laundry room, helped me retrieve the sweaters, and as I heard Monica's animated chatter coming from the back of the house, Don suggested to me that I should leave. I looked him straight in the eyes, and was met with a look of utter contempt. His voice was soft and controlled when he said it would be less fuss if I just went home with my things and forgot the whole incident. As if I were the one to blame! My guess was that his favorite couple brought nothing else but *my* things to share. Of course it is easier to give away things that do not belong to you! You can appear generous with property that isn't yours! I wanted to spit these thoughts at him, but I didn't. I left the house feeling like I was in grade school and the only one not picked to be on anyone's team at recess. I didn't expect adoration from the Meckleys, but this lack of understanding exceeded all expectations!

When the WOWs finished their year long "stand on the Word," they left their L.A. rented apartment by skipping out on the lease without notifying the landlord, and Monica's husband was fired from his job under a cloud of suspicious circumstances. Yet they were WOWs, and the apples of Don's eye. Regardless of this new wound, I foolishly continued to try and win my way back into the good graces of the Meckleys.

Chapter 13

Babysitter for Hire

If Jesus Christ had had the same source of soul life as all other men, he could not have legally redeemed man for he would not have been a perfect sacrifice. Similarly, if Jesus Christ had been God, he would not have legally redeemed man for he could not have willfully chosen to do so.

—Wierwille, *Jesus Christ Is Not God*

* * * * *

The incident at the Meckleys' caused a mixture of emotions for me. I knew I should forgive Don, but couldn't. I realized that I also couldn't approve of his style of leadership. My lack of respect and inability to forgive this man were ungodly traits and filled me with great guilt. This was a man holding a leadership position in a religious group I considered the only sanctioned, godly institution. Not getting along with one of TWI's esteemed leaders weighed on me heavily. I did not know how to deal with it.

As the summer changed into fall (a difficult thing to determine in L.A.), Bill and I continued to record and perform at Twigs, fellowship meetings, and other local Way functions. Bill had already recorded a cassette for The Way, but this new one promised to be quite an achievement for God, or so Bill believed it to be. Completion was difficult, because finding the funds to finish was slow going.

Although I tried to avoid meetings with Reverend Meckley, I kept in contact with his wife Cathy. I would sometimes call (I did notice it was usually me doing the calling) and ask biblical questions or just ask the advice of another mommy. On one occasion, I asked her what I could do about Mark refusing to tithe. My dear husband was generous to any number of charities, but staunchly refused to give 10 percent to TWI. I was able to give small amounts here and there, but when it came to tithing, the answer was a firm no.

Cathy told me that without Mark's permission, we really shouldn't tithe. It took both of us believing when we gave 10 percent. She also told me I could give in a different way. Her suggestion was babysitting. Wanting so badly to please and make up for our lack of faith by not giving what was expected of us, I reluctantly agreed. I was going crazy enough with my own two, and rarely getting out of the house as it was, but I didn't see another option. So, I became the Meckleys' babysitter.

Cathy soon began calling and asking to drop off her toddler and little baby quite frequently. Of course, my services were free. After several of these requests, there came a time when I was stuck, and turned to Cathy to help me with sitting.

The first time, she merely hesitated before saying yes. The second time I asked, her voice changed to a schoolteacher's tone when trying to speak to a particularly troubled student. Gently but firmly, she began to say that this was not what the arrangement was for. In essence, I was to be a sitter for her, not the other way around. This was to compensate for our lack of tithing.

I was so embarrassed. Another breach of biblical ethics? Couldn't I do anything right by God? I said I was sorry far too many times, and managed to get off the phone with hardly a trace of my dignity intact.

Upset and close to tears, I tried to think of what I could do to better myself for The Way. I couldn't tithe without my husband's permission, yet noticed what importance was placed on money within "God's family." I noticed that although Natalie was not in a leadership position, she was a very powerful woman (if your husband was a leader, the wife could be a co-leader; otherwise, I did not know of any women in a leadership position during those years). No matter where we lived, be it in Germany, Florida, or L.A., someone always knew Natalie. Money talked in this ministry, and although I loved my husband very much, I felt he was holding us back—me back—from ever really belonging. The Way greatly emphasized giving, giving, giving your money, money, money. Especially emphasized was the act of "abundant sharing," the amount given AFTER the expected tithe. I felt so inadequate. My goal of being a great woman of God began to fade right before my eyes.

I called Bill and Darlene to tell them what had happened. They both said that actually Cathy was the one that was wrong, not me. I felt a bit of relief, but was especially confused now. I began to believe them, and realized that as hurtful as this was, I would never be accepted by the Meckleys, so it was time to distance myself from them as best as I could. This was so upsetting to me. These were the people who were supposed to be my mentors, but now it seemed they were my enemy. I tried to convince myself to concentrate on the lovely people in my Twig, and quit trying to please my Branch leader, but conforming to the standards they required just didn't seem possible.

In the days that followed, I just said no to the repeated requests Cathy made for me to babysit. Eventually, she simply stopped calling. I felt as if a chunk had been taken from my heart. Although I could not bring myself to forgive Don, I *could* forgive Cathy. I had hoped that by our relationship, I could eventually patch things up with the Reverend Meckley. Now, this seemed impossible.

For the first time, I purposefully missed Way functions if I knew they would involve Reverend Meckley. The area ministry started really growing at this time, keeping Don very busy, so avoiding him was not a huge problem. The resentment towards Don began gnawing at me, although I refused to admit it at the time.

It wasn't until later, when I had the audacity to ask where the money we "abundantly shared" went to, that I had a *real* blowout with the Reverend Don Meckley.

Chapter 14

The Error of His Way

The Way is a fellowship of the followers of the Lord Jesus Christ for the manifestation of the more abundant life. A follower of The Way is filled with and manifests power from on high, holy spirit, and freely avails himself of fellowship meetings for spiritual nurture and growth. The Way fellowship is cemented together by the Spirit of God with each individual believer being transformed by the renewing of his mind according to the Word of God.

—A Way handout used as a recruitment tool

* * * * *

Bill and I continued to sing and record. An event featuring Don Meckley as the speaker was coming up, and we were allowed to sing for this fellowship meeting. We decided on four songs from Bill's new album, and gave Don a printed list with the words for his approval. He picked two, and those were the two we polished.

The night of the meeting came, and Bill and I were nervous as well as excited. It would be the first time anyone from leadership would hear us. We had barely stepped through the door when Don grabbed Bill and started hauling him to another room. I followed closely behind because I had a good notion of what Don was up to. He told Bill by phone earlier that day he had changed his mind, and wanted us to do another song. We weren't properly prepared. I told Bill to stand firm and, with all due respect, tell him we would do what was originally agreed upon. As I came to the threshold of the door, Don turned around and said that this would be a private meeting between him and Bill. I asked if it had anything to do with what we were singing that night. Reverend Meckley plainly said, "No," while slamming the door in my face.

Just before the door closed, I caught a glimpse of Bill's eyes as he stood behind Don. He was frightened. As much as I wanted to please God, I had come to the conclusion (at this point) that although God may have handpicked Wierwille, he obviously hadn't done the same with some of The Way ministers. It was the only possible explanation for the flaws that had become so obvious to me in the leadership of this organization. I firmly believed Don to be an inappropriate leader and that was the kindest thing I could say about him. Bill, on the other hand, felt just the opposite. Anyone in a leadership capacity for The Way International was directly in line to God, chosen by some revelation from on high. He lived his life to please these people, because he believed this would in turn be pleasing to God. He believed the chosen leaders to be holy, wise, and virtually without flaw, especially concerning ministry matters.

I waited for Bill to come out. When he did, he looked very uncomfortable to say the least. He told me we were to change the song, and that was it. I was absolutely furious. Not only did this self-styled reverend switch the songs on us knowing full well we were only prepared for the two he had originally chosen, but he also lied right to my face before closing the door on it! This was the final straw! It was all I could do to contain my hot Italian temper. The only reason I did not make a scene was because my dear friend Bill asked me not to. We did the two songs that Meckley picked, and I left early, knowing our first public appearance could have been far better.

I remember calling Natalie about all of this, and I must say I could detect a bit of impatience on her part. This too hurt my feelings. I thought she'd be in my corner. It was obvious she was no longer thrilled to hear from me, no less with yet another complaint. I vented with her, but did not feel the least bit satisfied. In fact, I felt worse. I hung up, angry and very frustrated.

It was during this time that I had been listening to a local radio station in Los Angeles. Every Sunday night, I faithfully tuned in to "Religion on the Line" with Dennis Prager. I had always been a letter writer and had already gotten a handful of my opinionated letters published in the local paper. I decided to write to Dennis Prager one night after calling in to the Sunday program.

I was trying to convince the panel of guests he had in the studio that Jesus Christ was not God. The group of various clergy from churches in the area completely dismissed my suggestion, claiming I was not a Christian. The only caller to back me up concerning the truth as I knew it at the time was from a caller who described himself as a Mormon. Realizing my beliefs coincided with a Mormon's disturbed me. Interestingly enough, this group is considered a cult by TWI, but I brushed it off, as usual, at the time. I considered being like-minded with this Mormon a mere coincidence and went into classic denial. I then wrote a six-page letter to Dennis Prager, detailing why Jesus Christ could not be God. My letters started in April of 1986.

In one of my first written contacts with Mr. Prager, I quoted from numerous books, especially the book by Wierwille, *Jesus Christ Is Not God*. In my closing, I even went so far as to say that my husband was a member of The Way. I am very humiliated to admit that I lied. My self-esteem was always low, and using Mark's credentials as a graduate of USMA at West Point was a method, or so I believed, of lending credibility to my letter. I was "merely" a housewife and felt I needed verification through my husband in order to be taken seriously.

I touched upon many points in my letter. One point, however, obviously caught the eye of Mr. Prager. It was a section concerning what Jesus said on the cross. An excerpt from my letter is as follows, lifted almost entirely from page 154 of *Power for Abundant Living*:

> Let me explain some inaccuracies I noted during your recent radio broadcast. It is important to correctly divide the Word of God [a phrase all Way leaders and members parrot], the Bible. Your guests quoted from Matthew 27:46, or Mark 15:34 when Christ said on the cross: "Eli, Eli, lama sabach thani? that is to say, My God, my God, why hast thou forsaken me?" King James Version.

The translation in the King James Version and obviously other Bibles has been from the Greek. However this is an erroneous translation. Christ spoke in Aramaic, or more accurately Syro-Chaldee. When the words are translated from Christ's language it is: Eli— God—but there is no Aramaic word like the word lama. There is a word lmna. Lmna is always a cry of victory, a declaration of "for this purpose" or "for this reason." The root of sabachthani is shbk. Shbk means "to reserve," or "to leave, to spare, or to keep." So the actual translation is "My God, my God, for this purpose was I reserved, for this purpose was I spared."

If we go by the Greek translation, then Christ believed God would forsake him. This contrasts with God's Word.

Mr. Prager's simple response was dated April 21, 1986:

I'm afraid King James is right. I know Hebrew/Aramaic and lama means "why." So I suspect Jesus, as a man, was asking God some question. (See Psalms 22:1.)

I was totally dazed as I read his letter. How could this radio personality be right and the Doctor mistaken? As quoted directly from the PFAL book: "The word Eli means "my God," but there is not an Aramaic word like the word lama."[13]

---

[13] Victor Paul Wierwille, Power for Abundant Living (New Knoxville,

These were Wierwille's written words. This exact teaching was taught in all of the PFAL classes. If it was an error, why was it still being taught?

Not being comfortable at the time with calling Don Meckley, I called The Way International headquarters in New Knoxville, Ohio. I was eventually patched through to Dick Herd in the research department. I had had other encounters with Dick when I sought material about The Way's stand on abortion (pro) and capital punishment (pro). His tone changed from its usual friendliness when I told him of my recent discovery, and asked if it was true. He confirmed my greatest fears, and after a brief conversation, suggested I take this up with my "local" leadership. Oh, sure. As if the great Reverend Meckley would just be a tremendous *wealth* of information concerning this topic!

I called Bill and Darlene, and Jim and Diane. They all expressed surprise, but were reluctant to believe Doctor was capable of making such a grave blunder.

I quickly wrote Natalie a letter dated April 27. In it, I explained everything that happened. It was clear that this was not welcomed news. My mother, who called frequently, called soon after Natalie had received the letter. Apparently Natalie was furious and embarrassed that her protégée had stirred this whole thing up. My mom told me that I should stop contacting Natalie completely. She tried to soften the blow by telling me how busy Natalie was with her local Twig, etc., which was called at that time The Way of New York, and that my constant need for advice was a burden on Natalie.

Of all the things that had happened to me since my involvement in The Way, this was by far the most

OH: American Christian Press, 1984), 154.

devastating. I was crushed. Not only was I unable to fit into the chosen family of God, but now a lifelong friend of the family was rejecting me! I asked Mom if Natalie had told her to say this, and she replied yes, but not exactly in the same words.

I was completely heartbroken. Soon, I received a letter from Lance Brigman, head of the New York ministry (Natalie had apparently passed on my letter). He admonished me for causing dissension and division, although he did not deny that error. He told me to be "like-minded" and to put my focus on these matters instead of the negative. Once more, a finger-wagging correction.

I didn't speak of this again until years later, when I came to the realization that being "like-minded" with Wayers meant believing doctrine contrary to the Bible.

Chapter 15

Mere Mortals

The Hoax of the Twentieth Century; The Myth of the Six Million.

Book circulated by TWI asserting that the Jewish Holocaust in Nazi Germany was a fabrication.[14]

"I was praying. And I told Father outright that He could have the whole thing, unless there were real genuine answers that I wouldn't ever have to back up on. And that's when He spoke to me audibly, just like I'm talking to you now. He said He would teach me the Word as it had not been known since the first century if I would teach it to others. Well, I nearly flew

---

[14] Encyclopedia of Cults and New Religions/Ankerberg/Weldon pg. 582

off my chair. I couldn't believe that God would talk to me…You've got to give me a sign so that I really know, so that I can believe…Let me see it snow…[the sky] was white and thick with snow."[15]

* * * * *

According to the research librarian at the Paulding County Library, there were no snowstorms during the months of September or October in Payne, Ohio in 1942.

* * * * *

My Twig with the Ballards shifted to a Twig at Bill and Darlene Anderson's house. Jim's job required too many hours, and the Twigs at their home became too much. Under Bill and Darlene's Twig, I was enjoying the same warm, tender fellowship. I was even able to nag Mark into taking the PFAL class at their home in March of 1987. The atmosphere was much less oppressive, and there were no limits on questions or note taking. The whole session ended with Mark *not* speaking in tongues. Due to his ever-demanding workload, he only followed it up by attending a mere handful of Twigs, and only because of my constant nagging.

The Branch leader of this Twig was Jack Thompson. His wife, Susan, and their four children were delightful. I especially became fond of Susan. My first Branch meeting under Jack Thompson was quite memorable. The Andersons had asked me to attend, but I had a terrible sore throat and

---

[15] This event supposedly happened October 5, 1942. Encyclopedia of Cults and New Religions pg. 584

didn't want to go. Knowing my absence would disappoint them, I made the effort to be there. After a short teaching by Thompson, I milled around a bit, trying to get to know some of the people. Other than Bill and Darlene, I knew no one.

I met a visiting Way "dignitary" from the Limb, who began a conversation with me. Soon into our talk, I mentioned that due to a terrible sore throat, I hadn't wanted to come, but was glad I had. He noticeably chilled. At first I thought it was due to the fact he didn't want to catch my germs but his reason soon became clear. Although he didn't say it in as many words, his impression was I shouldn't be sick in the first place, as this was a sign of "improper believing." One constant drumbeat throughout all Way teachings is "believing equals receiving." If I "believed" not to be sick, I shouldn't be. After his visible reaction, he turned abruptly, indicating an end to our conversation.

I was reeling from the embarrassment of it all and looked around sheepishly to see if anyone else had heard. My embarrassment was apparently a secret for the moment, so I quickly went over to Darlene to indicate I needed to leave immediately. She took this as a sign of my sore throat worsening, and ever the considerate friends, Bill and Darlene took me home within minutes of my request.

This episode was also pushed to the back of my mind, taking it as still another example of *my* inability to please the body of Christ. My mood in those days was far from upbeat. Although I was in denial about each incident, it was taking a toll on my emotional state. This constant feeling of falling short of the ideal was very psychologically damaging.

Shortly thereafter, I vented one night to both Jim and Bill during one Twig meeting that I had a problem with Wayers having to pay for any local or state-sponsored Way functions.

Despite my less than sterling standing with TWI, I just could not keep my mouth shut, and the mixture of guilt and insecurity made my stomach flutter as I explained my position. It seemed that all TWI events, or at least most, required a substantial fee. We were never treated, even on a national level. Local levels were continuously potluck. If it was a more formal type of function, a fee per person was always charged, and at one affair, our hands were even stamped! This prompted me to ask where the tithes went, as well as what The Way called "abundant sharing." Jim said I made a good point and would try to find out.

Within one week, I received a call from Reverend Meckley. He had been promoted because his area had grown in numbers. Surprise must have registered in my voice (he never called unless it had been to specifically return a call from me), so he told me it was just to say hello, see how I was, and to "bless" me.

Skeptical, I cautiously told him how thankful I was that he took the time from his busy schedule to check on me. I had recently given birth to my third child, a boy we named Alexander, in May of 1987. I wanted to believe that perhaps Don was extending the olive branch by calling to congratulate us on the birth of our son.

Eventually, I realized his true intent. I noticed he was asking questions concerning tithing and "abundant sharing" (what the Way defines as any donation above and beyond a 10 percent tithe). I then made the decision to confront Don about the secrecy surrounding TWI's assets. I asked for a full financial report of how The Way used our donations, because I found it odd that we always had to dig into our pockets and pay entrance fees for events.

"So, it's you who is stirring up trouble," he grumbled.

Instead of my usual guilt-ridden reaction, I became angry. I wanted to know what he meant by that and asked him directly. He ignored my question, asking if Bill had put me up to this. I assured him Bill had nothing to do with my search for information concerning Way finances and told him I found nothing wrong with my asking.

He ignored that comment, too, and insisted Bill and I were in this together, trying to cause trouble. I retorted that his ministerial duties obviously included giving members of his flock the third degree. He told me point blank that if I didn't like the methods "men of God" used to run TWI, why didn't I leave? I was shaking with rage when I told him that if anyone should be leaving, it should be him!

We hung up on each other and I immediately made numerous phone calls to Bill and Jim telling them what happened. Jim told me he never mentioned my name because he believed my question to be sincere, but suspected it would be met with this type of response. He wanted me to know that he tried everything to protect me. I believed him. My conversation with Bill was quite different.

He was angry that Don had said such things to me, yet sounded worried. I tried to convince him I took complete blame for everything said and that I cleared him of any suspicion, but this did not assuage Bill's fears. I didn't know it at the time, but the recording we had worked so hard on was now complete, and Bill was now awaiting approval from The Way leadership to distribute the finished product.

I got off the phone with Bill and decided to call Natalie, despite my mother's previous advice. I needed her now and was willing to take a chance that perhaps Mom had misunderstood.

Natalie listened attentively, then told me what I could say in response to Don's accusations. I took her advice and called Reverend Meckley back.

I told him (as Natalie advised) that since he was a man who serves God in a pastoral position, he should read 1 and 2 Timothy very closely. I also said I had the same amount of holy spirit as he or Dr. Wierwille had. His fury lashed out at me through the phone lines. He told me that I had *nerve* comparing myself to the handpicked man of God, Dr. Wierwille, and that he was fed up with my attitude...blah, blah, blah.

I cut him off. I told him I didn't have to listen to him any longer and promptly hung up on him.

He didn't call back, but decided to seek his revenge in a much more vicious way. I found out later that both Jim and Bill had received phone calls from Meckley. He believed Jim didn't plot this insubordination along with me, but oddly assumed Bill was a part of it. Bill refused to say much of anything to Don, and apparently tried to protect me by standing up to him concerning my questions about Way funds. He was labeled a coconspirator and for unknown reasons, Don's wrath became directed at Bill, almost certainly for the awful crime of agreeing with me. He told Bill later that week it was the decision of both him and David Shafer that not only was he unfit to represent The Way in recording, but he was not to perform musically at any event sponsored by TWI until further notice. Don might as well have told Bill that he'd be shot at dawn.

Bill's whole world came tumbling down around him. Within the next few weeks, our Twig at Bill and Darlene's evaporated, which sent me on an immediate search for a new one. Darlene indicated to me that Bill was obsessed with exposing The Way for the corrupt organization it was. After that, I lost contact with both Bill and Darlene for several weeks.

Also during this time, our Branch leader, Jack Thompson—whose parents were Corps, TWI's training for their "priesthood," and very high up in TWI leadership—suddenly left his wife of sixteen years. He moved in with a very wealthy older woman. Not only that, but he cleaned out his bank accounts. Susan called me one day to tell me this, and that she was going to be evicted onto the street with no money, no job skills, and four children. I had heard rumors about the Thompsons, but had no idea about the reality of the situation. She had nowhere to go, no car (Jack had taken it), and no one to help her move out.

She wanted me to go down to the welfare office with her so she could register for food stamps. I did. I watched her bravely clothe herself with dignity, despite her pain, for the sake of her four beautiful children. I was amazed by her courage and optimism in the midst of all of this personal and financial disaster.

While this chaos ensued, I noticed Jack and his mistress brazenly attending Way functions. I witnessed the leadership, including Reverend Meckley, embracing Jack as if he had done nothing wrong. Forgiveness was one thing, but this was acquiescence! He and his new girlfriend were popping up everywhere.

At this time, I was in almost daily contact with Susan and asked if she had been invited to any fellowships or meetings.

"No," she quietly replied.

It was just a matter of days before she was to move out of her home, and she had not received even one call from Don, Cathy, or anyone in leadership since Jack had left her. I was outraged and let Cathy Meckley know this. I phoned her on behalf of Susan. Cathy seemed quite annoyed that I was suggesting TWI had a responsibility to this Way-betrayed woman they weren't meeting. Her response was that the ministry wasn't "capable" of extending "financial charity," so what was it I expected anyone to do? I could hardly contain my disgust as I spat that the *least* they could do was find out when she was moving and offer to help. Cathy said she would discuss this with Don and promptly got off the phone.

As it turned out, Don and several others showed up to help Susan move. They loaded the rental truck for her and handed her the bare minimum assistance to move the five of them north to her mother's home. It was the last time Susan ever heard from the leadership of TWI. For me, it was the final straw and the last time I placed my faith in the men of The Way International.

* * * * *

While I was never an eyewitness or even knew firsthand of any sexual misconduct within TWI leadership, it was common. L. Craig Martindale, the handpicked replacement president of The Way International after Wierwille's death, used his position and power to take sexual advantage of women. Eventually, some brave woman brought a two million dollar civil lawsuit against him in Ohio. She alleged "sexual misconduct and abuse, assault and intentional infliction of fiduciary capacity, defamation of character and civil conspiracy. The suit also named several trustees and up to 50 other unnamed members of the Way leadership as defendants."[16] This lawsuit eventually forced Wierwille's successor to resign his position as president of TWI and a settlement was made out of court.[17] Subsequently, after this lawsuit was filed, other women have allegedly threatened lawsuits that have been quietly settled out of court as well. Men of The Way International certainly didn't act like men of God, or even as mortal men who deserved the respect they demanded from their followers.[18]

---

[16] William Laney, "Martindale Out at The Way," *Wapakoneta (Ohio) Daily News*, 27 April 2000.

[17] The current Way International President is Rosalie F. Rivenbark.

[18] For more information (and often graphic details) regarding sexual misconduct by Way leadership, read Karl Kahler's book, *The Cult That Snapped*, available through his Web site www.ex-way.com.

Chapter 16

Denial

"You too must follow God's truth as told in the Word of God. But if you think this is just Victor Paul Wierwille writing or speaking to you, you will never receive. If you know that what I am saying to you are words which the Holy Ghost has spoken and is speaking to you by me, then you too will manifest the greatness of the power of God."

Wierwille, *The New Dynamic Church – Studies in Abundant Living p. 116* American Christian Press, The Way International, New Knoxville, Ohio 45871

* * * * *

The Wrong Way

I began attending a new Twig at Dean and April Grumundi's house on the other side of the valley. Dean was a studio musician in L.A., getting enough steady work as a musician to support his family in a comfortable manner. He was once the drummer for a well-known pop music group, and The Way held him up proudly before believers like a trophy. He was also the drummer for Blastout, the band that won the music competition I participated in. I am loath to admit that I practically worshipped him. He and April were the Twig leaders, and although April was very sweet, I once again felt ill at ease in this new group of Way believers. It wasn't anything I could put my finger on, but I just didn't fit in.

Gossip started circulating about Bill within the new Twig. I was asked if I knew whether or not he had turned to drugs. I told them truthfully that I hadn't heard from Bill or Darlene. I am ashamed to say that I did not rally to their defense when I heard Wayers continue to downgrade Bill for his "improper believing." I merely would mumble something to the effect that they had always been nice to me.

No matter how many meetings I went to at the Grumundis', I never was able to feel comfortable. I hoped Dean, whom I not only considered to be an extremely talented musician but a solid man of God, would accept me into the fold. As it turned out, he, like Don, simply didn't like me. His forced politeness was almost like a slap in the face. I became unusually quiet at these Twigs. My attendance soon became sporadic, leading to guilt. Since the Grumundis were good friends with the Meckleys, I assumed my reputation had preceded me.

One particularly embarrassing incident happened after a Twig meeting. I had been talking to April on the phone about my concern that my tongues interpretation sounded stilted or forced. I wanted to be sure it was a natural occurrence from God. She said she would talk to Dean about it, and maybe after a Twig someday they could walk me through some practice tongues with interpretation. The Way believed that as long as there were three or more people,[19] tongues and interpretation could be performed correctly and in accordance with what the Bible said. Thinking the intimate setting of just the three of us would help with my nervousness, I eagerly agreed to a meeting.

The day came when April said I should stay after. I was thrilled. I would be getting some one-on-one time with my idol Dean, and I would also be polishing my "manifesting." I was both nervous and excited all at once.

After Twig, April indicated to me to hang around, and after the last person left, I could see Dean looking at me like I was some alien who had just made an unwanted landing in his living room. April, uncomfortably sensing this, quickly said to him, "Dean, remember I told you we would help Carol with tongues and her interpretation?"

Dean looked like we caught him in his underwear. He was totally uncomfortable. He said, "Uh...gee...uh, I was going to head out to the studio to go over something with our bass player..."

I stood up immediately, saying not to worry; we could do this some other time. April tried to talk Dean into it, and at the same time make me feel comfortable by trying to convince Dean they had just had this conversation, but this only succeeded in making me feel worse. I rarely blush, but I could

---

[19] *For where two or three are gathered together in my name, there am I in the midst of them.* Matt. 18:20 KJV.

literally feel the blood rushing to my face. I was so embarrassed by Dean's obvious distaste for doing anything with me, no less something so personal. The three of us stood awkwardly near the front door: me, trying to cheerfully say I understood and excuse myself, while April and Dean argued. I wanted to dig a hole right there, crawl into it, and never come up for air.

I eventually managed to convince April to stop trying to force Dean. With tremendous relief on his face, Dean whisked himself out the door, into his car, and out of the driveway before I could say, "believing equals receiving." April looked almost as mortified as I was. But my shame was mixed with the emotion, once again, that I was a square peg trying desperately to fit into a round hole. Why didn't anyone like me? My heart broke one more time and I quietly wept in my car on my way home.

It was about a year later when, without any warning, Dean came home one day, packed a bag, and left April and their only daughter. Thankfully, April's instincts told her to go home that day, or he would have taken his daughter with him. He claimed he needed to "find himself," and upon last report, he was trying to stay afloat in the music business out of L.A., not even staying in touch with his only child.

* * * * *

Shortly after the embarrassing episode at the Grumundis', Bill contacted me and asked me to come to his house to talk. The next afternoon, Darlene met me at the door of their large home looking terribly ill at ease. Bill introduced me to his sister, and for the first time, in their house, a feeling of dread started in the pit of my stomach.

Denial

Bill's physical appearance was unkempt and he looked agitated. His sister, Cam, looked calm and determined. I sat in a chair opposite Bill and Darlene, with Cam on my left. Without a hint of small talk, Bill told me Cam had been working at The Way International headquarters for a little over two years. Cam took over and immediately launched into a description of her time at the headquarters, which wasn't a pretty picture. She apparently had been treated like a slave. She told of how she was pressured into keeping all-night prayer vigils, only to be expected to scrub floors and clean bathrooms first thing in the morning. Evidently her pay was just enough to cover meals, although she was given free room and board for her numerous services. Her tasks varied: setting up for meetings, acting as a gofer, secretarial duties, night watch (although it was never made clear to me what it was they were keeping watch for), and manual labor. She also reported that adultery was a common and accepted practice among men in high leadership positions. She even bluntly stated that Dr. Wierwille had a particular liking for very young girls.

I was aghast. A tiny part of me started to believe what she said, but that prideful, stubborn, other side of me wanted to hold onto my foundation of beliefs in The Way and Dr. Wierwille. I couldn't possibly admit that I had been so wrong about so much. Even after all that had happened to me, I was not able to see The Way for what it was.

I looked at Bill, hoping to see even a glimmer of support for The Way, but he was nodding in agreement with everything Cam said. Darlene suddenly found something to do in the kitchen.

Cam told me some other allegations concerning what was going on at headquarters in New Knoxville, but I tuned her out. I started thinking that the gossip was true. Bill really looked as if he were doing some sort of drugs, and the fact that he was buying into all that Cam was saying was further proof to me that he had gone over the edge. Of course, I didn't conclude that Cam would have little reason to lie to me or try to mislead me, but because I didn't know her before this meeting, I simply dismissed her denunciation of The Way. In retrospect, I became a little frightened. A rug was slowly being pulled out from under me, and I didn't like the feeling one bit.

I stood up to leave. It was one thing to criticize, even denounce some of the people in leadership positions, but it was quite another to imply that the entire organization was corrupt. Bill leapt to his feet. He implored me to listen to Cam, to see this group for what it really was. He asked me to open my eyes. With my eyes wide open, I looked straight into his and said to my friend that I refused to believe that all of this was true.

Bill tried to argue with me for almost a half hour more, while Cam provided further details I don't remember. I ended by saying to Bill, sadly but firmly, "Bill, maybe this is all true, and maybe even someday I'll see what you both say as the truth, but I just don't believe that what has been said here can possibly be reality."

Bill followed me to the door, trying to convince me otherwise, but I managed to get out the door with numerous apologies. Darlene came out of the kitchen to say good-bye. I wasn't able to determine her stand on the issue at that time.

Gossip at the Grumundis' began to increase. Apparently, Bill was going around to the area believers, trying to convince each and every one that The Way leadership and the whole movement was corrupt. The entire community of believers in the area, with the exception of Jim and Diane, turned their backs on him. Don Meckley issued a warning to all the area believers that Bill Anderson was "marked to avoid." No one was to have contact with him whatsoever.

Way members were the only family and friends Bill knew. The rejection was more than he could take. This became evident some months later when Bill suddenly showed up at my house.

* * * * *

The doorbell rang, and when I looked through the front door peephole, I saw Bill standing on the stoop. I opened the door and warmly greeted him. The first thing I noticed was that he had dropped at least fifteen or twenty pounds. He was in his twenties, but already balding. He usually kept his thinning hair combed and fairly short, but it was now shoulder length, wild, and unkempt. His clothes were dirty, and hung loosely on him. Much to my shock, he even smelled bad. I assumed he had just come from work (he was successfully in business for himself as a professional window washer for local businesses), and figured that was the reason for his appearance. I invited him in for a visit.

He seemed very agitated. One of the first things he said was that Mark and I were the only people he could trust anymore. He sat at the kitchen table and began his tale, while I got us something to drink.

He started by telling me about immigrants coming over the border and trying to take over our American government. He had found some secret documents while on a job one day, and had already been to the FBI office to share this information with them. He also warned me not to tell Darlene any of this because she had an evil twin.

I was standing with my back to him at the kitchen counter, and with this last detail, paused. An evil twin? Something was terribly wrong.

I joined Bill at the table and we both sipped our drinks while he continued his disjointed thoughts. I used an opening in the conversation to gently suggest that perhaps Bill should talk to a counselor. He dove across the table, grabbed me around my throat with both of his hands, squeezing and shaking me while he accused me of being like "all the rest of them."

I managed to squeak out that I had obviously misunderstood and was sorry. This seemed to placate him, and he loosened his grip and sat back down. A childlike terror overcame me. I realized the kids and I could be in terrible danger, yet another part of me was looking at my old friend Bill, not wanting to believe any of this.

Thankfully, Mark came home from work. At first he didn't notice anything peculiar, but shortly into their conversation, Mark made a face to me as if to say, "What the heck is going on here?"

Somehow we got Bill out the door with promises to do our own investigation. When we closed the door behind him, I told Mark everything that happened. He rarely gave orders to me, but that day he forbade me to allow Bill into the house again, especially while I was alone with the kids.

In those days, never one to completely submit to authority, I ignored my husband's wise yet firm counsel. I spoke to Darlene, Jim, and Diane, and all three said that poor Bill had apparently turned to drugs. Darlene hardly recognized him anymore. During the next few weeks, Darlene and I reestablished our relationship.

One day Bill returned. Impulsively, I opened the door and let him in. He wasn't there more than five minutes when I realized my mistake. He asked to use the phone, which gave me a few minutes to try and decide what to do. Bill looked even worse than before, and wasn't even able to complete sentences. Once again, I became frightened for the kids and myself.

I managed to get to the phone by telling Bill I had to tell Mandy, a schoolteacher friend who lived only a few blocks away, that she couldn't come over. I must have sounded a bit out of touch with reality. She was aware of my previous encounter with Bill, so I started the conversation with:

"Mandy, you won't be able to come over today."

"Huh? I wasn't planning on coming over; what are you talking about?"

"No, Mandy, I really can't have you over today, it won't be possible, I'm sorry."

Bill began looking at me suspiciously. I began to sweat, drops trickling down my rib cage and temples.

"Carol, what are you talking about? I had…wait a minute, Bill's there, isn't he?"

"That's exactly right, Mandy. I'm really sorry, but maybe you can come over tomorrow."

"I'll be right over!" she replied and hung up the phone. Initially, I was relieved at this thought, but then became even tenser. What the heck could Mandy do? I was still hoping that she would think of something as a calm started to come over me. It was already dusk as Bill and I sat in the dining room at the back of the house, and I tried to sound interested in his ramblings. Within ten minutes (it seemed much longer), the doorbell rang. I asked Bill if I could answer it, but he believed the people who were after him were now at the door. Since the door had a peephole, he was able to see it was not his so-called pursuers. Mandy and another neighbor, Hal—a six-foot, three-inch, 250-pound fireman—were standing on my front porch. Bill said I could let them in, but not to tell them anything.

Mandy and Hal looked very worried as I answered the door (Mandy later told me that seeing no lights as they approached made them fear the worst). I let them in and Hal instantly stepped between Bill and me, extending his hand with an enthusiastic introduction of himself. He told Bill he was really glad to meet him and started to engage him in conversation. I almost slumped into Mandy's arms with relief. Bill seemed noticeably calmer, yet I detected something else in his eyes. I knew he would no longer trust me. We all went with Bill into the dining room while I got everyone something to drink. Bill and Hal made small talk while Mandy stayed close to my side.

When Mark arrived home about twenty minutes later, he was surprised to see Bill, but recovered quickly and started chatting with Bill politely before ushering him out the door. I couldn't thank Mandy and Hal enough. I was practically in tears as I led them to the door, thanking them all the way. When everyone left, Mark scolded me for letting Bill in the house in the first place. I vowed not to let it happen again; however, it was not the last time I saw my old friend. A few weeks later, Bill returned to my doorstep and the encounter was both frightening and heartbreaking at the same time.

Darlene called me a few days after my neighbors rescued me from Bill. We had a long, revealing conversation. She filled in some of the blanks as to why Bill had taken such a terrible turn.

As I had suspected, it started when Don told Bill he could no longer record or perform for The Way. Bill was devastated and devoted himself to researching TWI day and night, trying to find the proof that this organization was corrupt. Eventually, these late nights led to Bill taking aids to help him stay awake during his workday. With his background in illegal drug use, the over-the-counter pills soon led to larger doses, which then led to cocaine. At this point, she was deeply concerned that Bill had purchased a gun, and she didn't have any idea what he planned to do with it. She rarely communicated with him anymore, and she was actually frightened of this once sweet, gentle man. Concerned for my friend, I invited her to come over and she accepted.

Darlene arrived around four in the afternoon, and we talked for a few hours. She was exhausted. Bill was cleaning out all of their bank accounts and using it for drugs or only heaven knew what. She was about to leave and go to her car parked out in front when the doorbell rang. I looked through the peephole and saw Bill.

I told Darlene that Mark had forbidden me to allow him in the house, and Darlene was frightened enough not to want to go out and talk to him. I told Bill through the door that I couldn't let him in. He said he wanted to speak to Darlene. Darlene spoke through the door and told him she didn't want to speak to him and to just go away.

For the next few hours, Bill continued to ring the doorbell, pound on the door, and holler for us to let him in. He went to the windows in the front of the house, but I pulled the blinds. He continued to run around the house, yelling that he wanted to talk to Darlene. When it became dark, he then decided to go to the back of the house where the children's bedrooms were and started using his fists on the windows there. I tried to reach Mark, but he was tied up in meetings. When I was finally able to get through to Mark, the kids were hysterical and my nerves were frayed. Darlene and I decided not to wait for Mark to take the forty-five-minute trip home, and decided to call the police and have him removed. I told Bill I was doing this, but he continued his rampage.

The San Fernando Valley police arrived within minutes. I went out the front door to tell them what was happening, and Bill emerged from the side of the house, quiet, calm, and respectful. I was furious. This wasn't my friend standing in front of me, this was some stranger, and I wanted him arrested!

Bill was completely coherent, and acted normal as an officer questioned him outside, and another came inside with Darlene and me. I was shaking, and so was Darlene. As it turned out, the police didn't arrest him, but they told him to leave the premises. Bill did, and one of the officers stayed with us and spoke to us for a while. Mark came home just as he was about to leave. The police were extremely nice, and sorry they couldn't help further. Mark and I were concerned for Darlene's safety if she went home alone. We encouraged her to spend the night with us or with family, and she said she would go to family. That night, as Mark and I discussed what had happened, long after things had calmed down, I didn't realize that would be the last time I would lay eyes on Bill. Within a few months, we moved, and I wouldn't hear about Bill until I started writing this book almost seven years later.

Chapter 17

The Promise of Kansas

And if children, then heirs; heirs of God, and joint-heirs with Christ; if so be that we suffer with him, that we may be glorified together. For I reckon that the sufferings of this present time are not worthy to be compared with the glory which shall be revealed in us.
—Rom. 8:17-18 KJV

* * * * *

When we moved from L.A. in June of 1988, I remember saying I wouldn't even look in the rearview mirror, and I didn't. I am not condemning the City of Angels. The combination of the rejection by Way members, Mark's endlessly long hours with the Los Angeles Recruiting Battalion, and countless other things had taken an emotional toll on me. I now had three little babies, and although I had lost weight and routinely exercised, I still felt like a frumpy housewife. The kids and I hardly ever saw Mark, and I remained a single parent in a two-parent family.

Our clearing of the rented house we had lived in for over three years turned into a mini-nightmare as well. The landlord did not want to return our deposit. This man, who in three years' time had never received a late payment from us, had three months notice of our move, and even our leaving the house spotless, kept searching for ways to refuse our due money. He knew we absolutely had to leave that day to keep our plans before Mark reported to his next assignment. He also knew we *needed* that deposit money. At one point, with my friend Mandy at my side, I screamed at the landlord, "TAKE YOUR MONEY AND CHOKE ON IT!" Despite the fact he told every potential renter he would repaint the entire house for them, he made Mark scrub some imaginary fingerprints off the walls while we waited in the driveway. I think there must be a special room in hell for people like this. In spite of my outburst, we did get our deposit back that day, but it was like squeezing water out of a rock.

We drove caravan style: Mark in our ancient white Chevette, the lovely Mary in her little compact car, and me in our red minivan. Of course, I had the three kids with me, our two small dogs, most of the luggage, and *all* of the noise. Mary, a former military secretary turned civilian who used to work for Mark, had asked if she could drive with us because she was going to attend college in Pennsylvania, and didn't want to drive cross-country alone. Mary drove her compact car right along with us. She was young, firm, bright, and very beautiful. She also did not hide the fact that she had a big crush on my husband.

We began each day at two or three in the morning. Mark wanted the early start to avoid traffic and figured the kids would sleep most of the way. Also, traveling during the wee hours when the heat was less intense made it easier on the cars. I have enormous difficulty driving for long periods without dozing off, even during daylight hours. My stomach was raw from drinking Cokes and taking caffeine tablets to stay alert. By the third day of driving, I was a wreck.

That third morning, while I loaded the car with kids, dogs, and luggage, almost incapable of peering through my puffy, sleepy eyes, I noticed Mark rushing to help Mary pack her car. As he helped her load her single suitcase, I watched incredulously and with increased irritation, noticed that she looked great even at this ungodly hour! No wonder Mark was acting like a college freshman! The Jealous Monster began to rear its ugly head as I angrily signaled to Mark that I needed his assistance.

The rest of the trip was a nightmare. I believed Mark was more concerned with Mary's welfare, and in truth, far more attentive to her needs than mine. As the resentment swelled, I became increasingly distraught. In fact, if I had been supplied with a broom, I believe I could have flown my way to the east coast, cackling all the way.

We finally arrived in Lincoln, Nebraska, where we left the Chevette with my sister-in-law. Mark joined me in the minivan to continue our journey to the east coast to visit relatives. When we reached Pennsylvania, we came to Mary's destination. I waved good-bye with enormous relief and a bit of sadness. I actually liked Mary, but my insecurities and jealousy had ruined any possibility of ever developing any kind of relationship with her. Granted, I had some reason to be jealous, but not as much reason as I imagined. My insecurities bordered on psychotic by the time we reached my relatives in New York. I couldn't shake the impression that

Mark had put this young woman ahead of me, and had shamelessly flirted with her (according to my biased observations) the entire trip east. After visits to my family in New York and Mark's family in Michigan, we drove back to Lincoln, picked up the Chevette, and finally arrived at our new home, Ft. Leavenworth, Kansas.

During my visit to Latham, my hometown, I immediately arranged to go with Natalie to Lance Briggman's Twig a few blocks away. I anticipated enormous things; the buzz was that this guy was one hot teacher of God's Word. And judging from Natalie's devotion, he was dynamic.

The Briggmans' house was lovely and close to where I grew up. There were three different levels, and when I arrived with Natalie, we ran into ten or twenty people on each floor, friendly, and eager to meet me. Natalie didn't seem to show any impatience or didn't appear to distance herself from me as I had expected due to the earlier reports from Mom. I felt important, just because I was Natalie's friend, and anticipated a wonderful, fulfilling fellowship.

Reverend Briggman began the meeting with songs from *Sing Along The Way*. After an opening prayer, with the mandatory speaking in tongues and interpretation, he began teaching.

Perhaps I hit him on an uninspired day, but I didn't understand why this man was considered to be such a tremendous minister. It was a nice, pleasant teaching, but I must have expected something along the lines of Wierwille, because I was disappointed. He was soft-spoken, and nothing near what I had anticipated. In fact, I found him to be a bit strange. After fellowship, he directed his attention to me. When he addressed me, everyone in the room paused to listen.

In TWI, it seemed that whatever the leader did—as with diplomats or heads of state—the flock paid rapt attention.

"So, this must be Carol." He then added, "Remember me to Dorothy."

I stood there awkwardly; I had no idea what the heck he was talking about. He repeated the same four words without explanation, evidently anticipating a reaction from me. My confusion now became a weighty presence in the room as my embarrassment increased.

I was quite certain no one else knew what he meant either, but most still stood with frozen smiles on their faces, looking to me to end the uncomfortable silence that seemed to have a physical presence in the room.

Finally, in complete exasperation, Briggman said, "You ARE going to Kansas, aren't you?"

"Yes..." was my hesitant reply.

"Well, remember to say hi to Dorothy for me, you know, *The Wizard of Oz*? Geez..." He moved past me, obviously irritated that I had not understood his joke.

Once again, I felt removed from the people I longed to be a part of. Once again, I had done something wrong. I could not please these people, even though it was my ultimate goal. I wanted to be one of them. I wanted to fit in, and not *just* fit in, I wanted to be admired by them. I wanted to set a perfect example and be looked upon favorably by every Wayer I met. I was amazed they didn't spit on me...

The remaining believers acted coolly to me until I finally left. No matter where I went, it seemed I was simply an outcast with these people. I felt unable to please God and his chosen children. I drove back to my Mom's feeling grievous despair, but held out hope that something good would happen once we arrived in Fort Leavenworth. After all, didn't Dorothy's luck change?

BOOK III

THE WAY OUT

Chapter 18

Shaking the Tree

Many scriptures have been wrongly used to substantiate the doctrine of "God the Son" by those not adhering to the fundamental principles of Biblical interpretation.

—Wierwille, *Jesus Christ is Not God*

* * * * *

Fort Leavenworth is an older army post outside of Leavenworth, Kansas, near Kansas City, and along the banks of the Missouri River. When we drove through the gates that day in 1988, the road was tree lined, the sky was bright, and I had a feeling of expectation. It was a fresh start, and I was optimistic that things would be better for us at Ft. Leavenworth.

Our government quarters in the Kickapoo division were quite small, no larger than nine hundred square feet. But the two-story units were in a very nice location, with a backyard overlooking a beautiful wooded area. It was a quiet cul-de-sac, and we immediately began meeting our friendly neighbors the day our moving van arrived.

During our first year, we made some lifelong friends. I didn't know it at the time, but the bonds we established were deep and lasting. Our husbands all attended the Command and General Staff College, and although the work was intense at times, generally their hours weren't too bad. Mark, along with some of his peers, also worked to get his master's degree. The hurt from our cross-country trip, combined with my utter resentment that Mark was getting his master's while I could not, was causing a welling bitterness inside me that I did not realize.

Alex had just celebrated his first birthday, and soon began a campaign, most certainly plotted by Satan himself, to drive me into an early grave. He was willful, extremely curious, and very active. While he was awake, I had zero rest. I was, however, fortunate to have numerous understanding mommies to unload upon. Usually, during the lazy summer days, we would place lawn chairs in front of the home of the day, bring out our baby monitors if our precious ones were napping, and have long visits. This became a daily occurrence, and the husbands would usually join us as we often sat out front and visited through the evening and night.

Despite the relaxed atmosphere and socialization, I was deeply unhappy, but couldn't understand why. By all appearances, we were a perfect army family, and I, the devoted and adoring wife. Things, as they say, aren't always what they seem.

I had started getting headaches, and apparently was extremely allergic to Kansas and bordering Missouri. I continually developed upper respiratory ailments. I would no sooner finish the antibiotic than new cold symptoms would develop. I usually ended up with bronchitis, which would occasionally lead to pneumonia. I would cough so hard sometimes, I felt certain I'd have a stroke. These coughing fits usually occurred at night and aided in keeping me from getting a full night's rest. This was not exactly an uplifting existence.

During our first year, we met a couple, Jonathan and Betty Abernathy, who were Twig leaders. Jonathan was an army lawyer and Betty was one of the sweetest people I have ever known. They had no children, and were a musically talented team. Betty was the first Way person I met who was openly critical of the leadership. We traded stories about our dissatisfaction with the methods Way leaders used.

I attended a few fellowships at the Abernathy home where Reverend David Stanton officiated. My initial reaction again was that I had finally found my church family. The Abernathys were generous hosts, and the members of the small Twig practically dripped warmth. However, my life revolved around my new Kickapoo friends, so I did not attend Twig faithfully.

I did go to a huge gathering of TWI in Kansas City, Missouri. The atmosphere was similar to the usual Way events where higher leadership were present—oppressive and stifling—but for the most part, it was far less intense than the meetings I had previously attended. There was more of a worship environment.

There was one major change at this event: we didn't have to pay anything to attend. I wondered if my disruptive questions had shaken the leadership a bit. The atmosphere was as if some important celebrity was going to be speaking. Designer suits and self-important men lolled about with smug looks of disapproval on their faces. I can't recall who spoke, but we were there to "fellowship with like-minded believers in the Kansas area." I barely recall what was taught either, but I do recall something that happened afterward.

Betty and I were milling about when we ran into Audrey, a lovely lady Betty knew from a different Twig in another part of the country. Audrey was an intelligent, impressive woman with huge, intense hazel eyes that made you want to hang on her every word. She owned her own catering business, and I was instantly impressed with her casual sense of humor and warmth.

Betty told Audrey about some stomach problems she had been experiencing and asked Audrey to pray for her. Without blinking an eye, Audrey bowed her head in prayer for her friend.

I do not recall her exact words, but I do remember she began praying that the Father touch Betty's uterus and that the pain Betty was feeling would be removed by the power of Jesus Christ. She also said something about a blockage and that this too would be healed in Jesus' name. I thought Betty must have told her about what was going on.

When Audrey finished, Betty looked at her, stunned. Betty had not told Audrey any specifics about her condition, yet Audrey had known exactly what was wrong with her. Betty had just been told that morning that she had fibroid tumors on her ovaries that were causing the pain and the blockage. There is NO WAY Audrey could have known this. I was in awe and once again saddened at the same time that this "wonderful and powerful ministry" was run by such crackpots instead of women like Audrey.

Some weeks later, there was another large meeting, once again in Kansas City. Betty asked me to attend with her, but I declined. I told her to find out what was going on, because somewhere deep inside, I felt something was brewing. I had very little basis for this feeling, and it was just that: a feeling. Though distancing myself from The Way at this time, I picked up on things Betty would say about her Twig leadership meetings, and also some rumblings among the believers I had met since moving to Kansas. I believed there was infighting and tension since Wierwille's death, and I thought that the ministry was starting to fall apart at the seams.

As it turned out, my instincts were correct. Betty called me the moment she returned from the meeting. Reverend Stanton had submitted his resignation, explaining to the believers present that there had been a major flap in The Way International, and that Ohio leadership was calling for mass resignations. It was a far-reaching shake-up and despite my many questions—as well as the innumerable questions of others in the organization—the leadership was remaining tight-lipped about why all this occurred.

I was deeply shaken. It was one thing when I *chose* not to attend Twigs, but it was quite another not to have any available. My stomach became queasy with the shock of it all. The ministry broken up? Where would I go to hear the "pure Word of God"? Where would I go for "like-minded" fellowship? Who could I follow as a leader in God's "chosen" organization? I was quite upset. What I didn't realize was just how deeply troubled I became, and ultimately didn't recognize the danger signs.

Betty assured me that we would continue our Twig, but I sensed that she too was quite shaken by the news. We both felt David Stanton was a very competent man of God, and had understood his ministry to be the best in all of our travels. We ended our conversation on a very somber note.

I didn't tell Mark or my friends. No one knew I was a member of The Way. I managed to block this event from my mind as best as I could, and threw myself into a very active social life. Our entertainment revolved around planning and doing things on the weekend with our friends. Even if we all didn't actually go out anywhere, we spent just about every single weekend with our neighbors, partying with some light drinking. Rarely did anyone become intoxicated, although there were occasions when someone would stagger home.

During a trip Mark had to take to Florida as part of his school training, I was upstairs, getting Alex up from his nap. As I held him on my right hip, I started down the wooden staircase of our quarters. Suddenly, my right foot slipped out from under me, and with my left hand, I grasped the railing as my lifeline. I gripped the railing with all my strength, and this prevented me from falling headlong down the stairs. However, in doing so, this left my left leg in place, while the rest of my body flailed around, attempting to gain my balance as I fought to keep hold of Alex.

I managed to stay on my feet, but knew I had done something to my left hip and lower back. Within a few hours, I was in agony and couldn't even stand up straight. I drove myself to the emergency room, and was barely able to get myself through the ER doors.

After an examination, I was told I had a rotating iliac and a pinched sciatic nerve. In other words, I had wrenched my hip, and the pain could be temporary or extended. I was manipulated by an orthopedic surgeon and sent home.

I was certainly feeling better when I left the ER, but soon after arriving home, the pain became intense. Within an hour, I was on the floor, unable to get up, screaming in pain. My next-door neighbors happened to hear my cries, and as

Christina took care of the kids, Dick carried me up the stairs to bed. I called back the doctor who had treated me. He had neglected to mention that if I experienced any pain, I should remain flat on my back with no movement except when absolutely necessary, for at least five days straight. Mark had to come home, and for five days and nights, the pain was excruciating, and that is putting it mildly. Even childbirth was not this intense! The ER doctor told me during that second call that I may have caused some serious damage to my nerve, and only time would tell how much impairment would result. Not the words I needed to hear, to say the least.

Although I stayed on my back faithfully, except to use the bathroom, my recovery was slow. Even after two weeks, I was more mobile but still in considerable pain. With the combination of the pain in my lower back shooting down my left leg without warning, and my constant illnesses, my physical pain lead to an ever increasing emotional pain.

I tried to overcome my growing discomforts by hosting a Bible study in my home, inviting my good friends so that I could foist Way doctrine on them (without letting them know it was Way doctrine). I taught these Bible studies once a week, and although I didn't touch on the controversial issues The Way taught, I did use *The Power for Abundant Living* book almost word for word. I didn't get very far. After our fourth meeting, my friends politely decided this wasn't for them. Once again, I felt adrift in my spiritual life. Despite trying other churches, I couldn't sit through a service without becoming offended by their "wrong" teachings from the Bible and eventually gave up even trying.

For the rest of that year, I was constantly sick, adding occasional migraines to my list of maladies. When Mark was one of fifty officers selected from over 350 for SAMS (School for Advanced Military Science), I met the honor with mixed emotions. This would mean another year at Ft. Leavenworth, and all of our friends leaving us behind. On the other hand, it was a tremendous honor to be chosen for this school. In my typical army wife style, I met the challenge with optimism despite my body falling apart at the seams.

When June came, our friends started leaving one by one. It was an especially emotional time for me. I felt so distant from Mark, inwardly blaming him for all of my woes, including the breakup of The Way. I felt deserted. My life was on hold, but my friends and my husband moved on. I had stopped exercising, and was lumpier and heavier than I had ever been. Alex was impossible; he now refused to take a nap, climbing out of his crib every time I put him in it. He even started climbing out of it in the middle of the night, leaving his bedroom, and had tried on several occasions to go out the front door to wander the neighborhood, as was his trick during the daylight hours. I was forced to sleep lightly so that I could catch him before he would actually make it out of the door. I finally asked the military police if I could put a chain lock on the outside of my son's bedroom door so that he couldn't wander during the night. This was the only way I was able to get any sleep at all, because although this stopped Alex's midnight raids, it did not prevent him from waking at four or five in the morning, ready to greet the world. I was running on little sleep, and woke almost every morning unable to stand up straight. I was suffering from intermittent, blinding headaches and constant upper respiratory problems. I was bulging out of my clothes, and started noticing that my hair was beginning to turn gray. Worst of all, I had no church to attend. I was deeply unhappy, but somehow, remarkably, didn't realize it on the surface.

My inner turmoil surfaced with the arrival of our new neighbors, and a dangerous attitude I began to adopt.

Chapter 19

A Shocking Confession

If there arise among you a prophet, or a dreamer of dreams, and giveth thee a sign or a wonder, And the sign or the wonder come to pass, whereof he spake unto thee, saying, Let us go after other gods, which thou hast not known, and let us serve them; Thou shalt not hearken unto the words of that prophet, or that dreamer of dreams: for the Lord your God proveth you, to know whether ye love the Lord your God with all your heart and with all your soul.

—Deut. 13:1-3 KJV

* * * * *

I decided one way to change things was to work out at the gym on all the modern equipment they had. This became my new obsession. I never missed a workout day; I exercised sometimes five—but never less than three—days a week, a few hours each time. I molded my petite body into a lean, toned, physically fit machine. I was extremely proud of the results that began to show within two weeks. I looked great, and I knew it. I also began physical therapy sessions with a certified army physical therapist. In three weeks, he had my back good as new. I felt as if that whole year of on-again, off-again suffering was decades behind me. I was a new woman!

I soon began an unhealthy relationship with any man that would return my flirtatious ways, and dressed, quite frankly, like a tramp. At the time, I of course didn't see it this way. I wore micro miniskirts and body hugging, clinging clothes. I believed I was merely showing off my new body and that there was nothing wrong with this. Consciously, I was not after any man, yet unconsciously, I needed the approval of someone...*anyone*. Deep within my hurting heart, the rejection of The Way was a step into the deep end for me and I needed to fill that void. I honestly believed flirting was all just harmless fun. I was in complete control. My intention was just to have a bit of innocent amusement.

As it turned out, my fun took a very evil and nasty turn when the holidays approached. One terrible memory that will not soon fade is an evening at a formal bash. A friend asked me to "distract" her husband so that she could "have some fun" with someone else who also happened to be married. This was the disastrous opening of a door that should have remained tightly closed. Soon thereafter, when many of us were pretty sauced during the New Year's celebration, I made a blatant play for this friend's husband. I knew it was dangerous, and despite this, I pursued this man, Danny, as if he were my last hope for happiness. He hardly had a chance. Although this relationship did not advance to physical consummation for many months, the adultery had already been committed in my mind and heart as I gave what I thought was love to this man, via long telephone conversations and secret meetings in public so as to give the appearance of innocence.

I replaced the god I had made of The Way organization with this man, and believed that in this one person lay all the answers I had been searching for my whole life. My contempt for my husband was barely hidden. I became cold and distant, dreaming of ways to easily end our marriage. Danny had a family of his own, and the sin we were committing had a devastating effect on us, as well as our families.

In late February, I decided to tell Mark that I wanted out of our marriage. I had never felt assured of his love, believing that I had always loved him more than he loved me. I figured that this might even be a relief for him and that I shouldn't have too much of a problem getting the divorce I believed I wanted. As it turned out, this wasn't going to happen. Although I had no plans to actually get together with Danny—he was married with children he was devoted to and had never made any real attempt to express interest in a future with me—I still wanted out of my marriage. I figured I was still young, and if I were free, this would enable Danny to make up his mind much more quickly about leaving his wife.

Mark had other ideas. He was extremely shocked by my confession. From that moment on, he made it very clear that he was willing to fight for our marriage. I didn't want that! In the wee hours of the morning, after telling him, Mark woke me to show me something. He could speak in tongues. There was no denying that I believed this to be a true sign of a believer—that if one could speak in tongues, then they were saved, period. I was cold and unfeeling as he said that he was willing to do whatever it took to put our marriage back together. Quite frankly, I did not believe him.

The Wrong Way

As I lay in bed with my back to him, arms folded across my chest in a posture of defiance, I thought, "This doesn't matter. I want a divorce!" I also remember, even more clearly, a voice inside my head that said, "You must not divorce your husband."

I was so shocked by this tiny voice that I sat bolt upright, but immediately caught myself and stubbornly refused to believe what I heard. I told Mark that it was too late. That I'd been telling him for years I wasn't happy, and that we should go to counseling, but he had always refused to go. Sometimes, I would even go by myself. It was simply too late! I wanted out while I was still young. I needed someone who wasn't afraid to show me how much he loved me. I needed someone who was willing to share a life with Christ (ironically I believed at that time that I needed a divorce to do this), and I needed someone who hadn't hurt me with all those years being distant and unaffectionate. I wanted to live, and I didn't want it to be with him. I justified what I was doing to Danny and Danny's family (although his wife did not suspect anything) by believing that we just found each other too late. I thought it to be a mistake in timing, and I didn't want anything to stand in the way of my newfound happiness. I believed Danny could make me happy and at peace. I wanted to spend the rest of my days with Danny, the only man who had ever made me feel beautiful, smart, funny and desirable, and so complete. I firmly believed by now that I had never even loved my husband and that he only wanted our marriage to stay together out of some kind of pride thing.

I wanted Danny and a life with him, no matter what it took, no matter how long I had to wait. I wanted this for myself, no matter what.

A Shocking Confession

I confided all of this to a dear friend, Daphanie Paisano. Daphanie, one of my Kickapoo neighbors the previous year, was a new Christian at the time. She told me that what I wanted to do was wrong. I also confided in Audrey, the lovely lady I had met at that Kansas meeting who had prayed over Betty. I felt her maturity in the Bible was essential to help me make decisions. I used every single excuse to demonize Mark so that I could justify leaving him. Both Daph and Audrey told me essentially the same thing: you mustn't leave your husband. There isn't anything that God can't fix, and there are children involved on both sides. Most of all, I had to stop what I was doing with another woman's husband.

My emotional state at this point was on the critical list. I fluctuated between feeling I absolutely couldn't take another breath if I didn't speak with Danny, and feeling, when I did, a high that must rival what a cocaine addict feels after their fix. Then I would drop to the lowest of lows when I wasn't with him or talking to him. The guilt was maddening. I ran from God at every turn. I honestly began to avoid the mirror because that meant I might catch a glimpse of myself doing things I never thought I would do. I was nothing, yet I thought if I could only divorce, I could be *something* with this man I felt without any doubt I HAD to have. I was losing weight rapidly, my hair started falling out, and I couldn't sleep through the night unless I was completely drunk.

Something made it through to my brain, and I eventually agreed with Mark that I should at least try to give my marriage a shot, if only for the kids. I made it *abundantly* clear that they were *the only* reason I remained in the marriage. I believe the Lord started showing me in many different ways what a divorce could do to my children. I reasoned that I needed to go to counseling and give it my very best shot before I gave up completely on the marriage. This time, Mark not only agreed to go, but he was enthusiastic. I still held steadfastly to the notion that he didn't love me, and was doing all of this out of a sense of pride. Oh, I knew he was greatly *fond* of me, but I didn't believe for one moment that he could be capable of giving me the love that I so needed. I continue to use the term *needed* because I was consumed with the love portrayed by pop culture—from all the love songs and movies and books—that I expected Mark to give me. It was this mutated version of love that I thought could replace the total emptiness I felt after leaving The Way. It was this warped love that I thought could be the answer to all of my dreams and fill the hole in my heart that had remained empty throughout my life. When Mark didn't give this to me in the early years of our marriage (no person can make another feel whole), I started my search and found The Way. When The Way fell through, the search intensified and the hole in my heart enlarged. I thought that through another man, I could finally fill this hole. I also believed that finding my dream man would be the answer to everything. Absolutely everything.

I so foolishly thought and believed very strongly that the solution was in another woman's husband. The guilt and repulsion I felt towards myself did not override my desperate need to fulfill this dream of having a soul mate for life. I had completely made up my mind that my need to have this man was the most important thing in my life, and I wouldn't settle for anything other than my goal of ending up with him as my husband. I was aware that he may not have shared this dream—willing to give up everything to be together—but that was all right. I would wait, believing that some day we would be together. It was the only possible solution I could live with at the time.

It soon became clear that Mark had other plans for our marriage and me. It began with our counseling sessions. First, I found a minister through the army chaplain system whom I met with alone. He was horrible. From the moment I stepped into his office, he began to scold me. Though he spoke in truth, his delivery was horrendous. I felt battered and bruised when I left his office after one hour. Mark and I decided to try someone else (although at first I used that disastrous meeting as an excuse to forgo any further counseling), and found a gentle yet experienced army chaplain who also met with me alone for our first meeting.

He seemed to understand fully what I was trying to tell him (I didn't say I was interested in another man at that first meeting). Mark was a type something-or-other, and had thus far been unable to give me the attention and affection I required. I, on the other hand, coming from a broken home, with a broken heart and now a broken faith (although The Way, at this point, did not come into any sessions), made it impossible for anyone, even my husband, to give the obligatory Band-Aid necessary to mend my open wounds. I was a basket case, and looking for a quick fix wasn't going to do the job.

I had been replacing one god for another throughout my life, and my latest god turned out to be one of the most damaging gods of all. I honestly believed that the breakup of my marriage, and somehow marrying this already married man, would be my heaven on earth. I was very wrong, and the problem became how to give up this dream-turned-nightmare.

Chapter 20

Starting Over

Humble yourselves therefore under the mighty hand of God, that he may exalt you in due time: Casting all your care upon him for he careth for you.

—1 Pet. 5:6-7 KJV

Now faith is the substance of things hoped for, the evidence of things not seen.

—Heb. 11:1 KJV

* * * * *

The counseling with the chaplain started going well, although I stubbornly refused to admit it. Every once in a while, I would recall that clear, small voice that night when Mark showed me how willing he was to try and save our marriage. I still wanted what I wanted—the only man I felt understood me—but just hadn't figured out how to get around *his* spouse and kids. Blessedly, his wife never suspected a thing.

Each session, now with Mark present, was an emotional roller coaster. I would literally sit there with my arms folded across my chest, trying to ignore the fact that Mark was obviously trying to do whatever it took to put our marriage back together. I only wanted to believe he was doing it out of a sense of pride, and not because he really loved me.

During this time, I told Mark I was not in contact with Danny, but the truth was we were talking by phone constantly. I decided I needed some time away, and impulsively flew to Ft. Benning, Georgia, where my former Kickapoo friend, Daphanie, and her family now lived. Mark figured I wouldn't contact Danny from there, so this trip seemed a good idea to him. He knew there wouldn't be any secret meetings or even phone calls to Danny at my straight-as-an-arrow friend's house. He was right.

I stayed ten days, and although there was contact, it was with Mark's permission. In my friend's home with a strong Christian atmosphere, I decided to give up Danny, and really make an effort to give my marriage another try. I didn't come to this conclusion overnight. I certainly had a bunch of people praying for me, but it was with determination that, under her roof, I called Danny to tell him that all of this must end. Staying in their home was a healing and learning process. I watched a Christian family function as a cohesive unit, and longed for this to happen with mine. The love the Paisanos extended to me was unconditional, accepting (despite what I was guilty of), and safe. I immersed myself in their children, and the atmosphere of a Christ-centered family. I began to feel hope.

I was primarily separating myself from Danny for the sake of my children, not to save my marriage. Despite the wonderful fellowship at Daphanie's and all that I experienced, I couldn't take it home with me, and more importantly, I couldn't absorb it inside of me. I still foolishly believed I no longer had any feelings left for my husband. I guess I hoped that if I obeyed God, and didn't divorce Mark now, God would give me the desires of my heart, and that was to someday be with Danny...maybe after the kids grew up. I made what I thought was a deal with God. For the time, it was a great step in my recovery.

After my trip and partial emotional healing in Georgia, I came back and began to get ready for our move to Ft. Drum, New York, in June. My good intentions melted away, as Danny and I continued to contact each other via the phone. I am loath to admit it, but the fact of the matter is, I believed that this forbidden "love" was what gave me the strength to go on. My favorite pastime was to listen to MTV, pick out the popular love songs, and apply them to my situation. When they didn't have enough sappy songs, I turned full force to country music to fill the gap. I either sat in front of MTV, watching it for hours, or I played my CD boom box. I was never without my mood-controlling music.

The time came for us to move. Deep down, I believed that removing myself from this place would be a relief. On the surface I suffered the pain of separation. I said my final good-byes to Danny, as always, via the phone. I wanted to die, yet deep inside, I felt hope and a sense of relief. Danny was going overseas, and I figured there wouldn't be any way to "safely" contact him, so I thought quitting cold turkey was the best thing for everyone. At this point, I realized that if I wanted to make my marriage work *at all*, it was going to have to be without Danny in my life. This may seem like a *glaringly* obvious detail to everyone else, but understand I was addicted to this man as if he were a drug. I had placed all of my hopes and dreams on having a life (someday) with him. Giving this up was, at that time, one of the most difficult things I had ever done. I couldn't stand the thought of never hearing from him again, and supposedly, he felt the same, but I still asked him not to contact me for a minimum of three months. He told me that this would not be easy, but he promised he would do this. I did not give him a forwarding address and didn't get one for him. I felt safe, at least for a little while, from myself.

Moving to upstate New York in June of 1990, outside of a place called Watertown, seemed appropriate. Near the Canadian border, it was far from Kansas, near my home of Albany, and the air was fresh and clear. My allergies seemed to improve, and so did my headaches. The northern air was refreshing, and it set the stage for a brand-new start. I felt more affection for Mark, but that was as far as I would let myself feel. Mark, on the other hand, was endlessly patient with me. The old Carol, previous to Kansas, was always hanging on him, despite his inability to show outward affection. Now, the tables were turned. The counseling sessions had really changed him. He wasn't the least bit shy about showing his deep feelings for me. I, on the other hand, had taken the cold fish approach. I just wasn't going to trust that he had changed. He had done this in the past—changed, and then gone right back to the same old, same old. I wasn't ready to trust him, not yet anyway. I was still reeling from the false feelings of losing the only man I thought I had ever loved. I hadn't realized that my heart was an unforgiving one, a heart God would heal in the coming months.

Chapter 21

An Open Door

I can do all things through Christ which strengtheneth me.
—Phil. 4:13 KJV

* * * * *

Almost three months to the day had passed since leaving Ft. Leavenworth. Although I had fooled myself into thinking I had cut all ties to Danny, I left a door open. I had given him a friend's address, and this was ultimately the way he first contacted me.

She read the letter to me over the phone, and then mailed it to me. I felt dread in one respect, knowing deep down the consequences of allowing this letter to come into my hands; and yet, I couldn't stop myself. The day arrived when his letter came, short, but to the point, and I read it with shaking hands. My overblown romantic view of what "love" was kicked into full gear as the floodgates opened, and I knew that we would be in contact once again.

I obtained a post office box, and sent a letter to an address he had given me. I gave him my phone number, and thus began secret calls back and forth. I even got my own phone card. The calls weren't frequent—neither of us could afford the expense—but they were enough to keep this foolish notion alive that I could live a double life.

Mark noticed I was becoming even more distant. He intensified his loving, patient, yet persistent approach. His attention and tenderness were remarkable. Almost immediately upon arriving in Ft. Drum, we began attending a Pentecostal church in Watertown. Pastor Mike Bartholomew and his wife, Connie, welcomed us into their church family with open arms. While I immediately felt genuine warmth from them, I was not ready for a mainstream church, and held steadfastly to the teachings of Victor Paul Wierwille. Pastor Mike used a King James Version of the Bible, as did The Way, so that helped ease my anxiety. Pastor Mike was very familiar with the teachings of The Way, due to some longtime parishioners having once been members. I sensed that he would go easy on me. We decided to make Faith Fellowship our church home, despite the fact I was hesitant about a church that believed in the Trinity.

To my delight, Jonathan and Betty Abernathy had preceded us to Ft. Drum. From the moment we arrived, a bond developed between Betty and me that I hadn't been able to feel with a friend in a long, long time. There was something different about this friendship. She was like an angel that God had sent to me. I confided my deepest, darkest secrets to her. She praised me and adored me like Danny did. She thought I was the greatest thing on the planet, that my talents were unlimited, and despite the grave sin I was guilty of, she loved me unconditionally. This was not an unnatural love by any stretch; it was the love of a dear, sweet, giving friend. Our "like-minded" beliefs only seemed to cement this impenetrable friendship. In a year's time, we never had a disagreement.

As Betty and I grew closer, I began distancing myself from Daphanie. She insisted on telling me, often gently but sometimes forcibly, I had to give up The Way teachings AND any thoughts of being with Danny. I could not fathom giving up The Way, and in my heart, even though I knew at this point I probably could never have Danny, I didn't want to let go of that dream either. I felt that if I just "did my part" in the marriage, someday I could have the man that I believed was the answer to it all for me.

Remarkably, although her lifestyle paralleled Mother Teresa's, Betty understood me, and never made me feel uncomfortable. She adored me, as I adored her. I didn't realize it then, but God had given me someone in my life who loved me the way I perceived Danny did, only this was a normal, healthy relationship, without sin. God gave me Betty to fill the empty holes in my heart for a time, until I was ready to face the cause of these holes. While God prepared me to face the depth and breadth of these chasms, he provided me the unconditional, Christlike love of a cherished friend, Betty, and the wisdom and guidance of a patient pastor, Mike Bartholomew.

Although I drifted from the friendship, Daphanie still called periodically to check up on me. Our conversations were usually stilted—she, knowing I was keeping things from her, me, believing she simply didn't understand me. I attributed it to the fact we weren't "like-minded" in our beliefs. Betty and I, of course, assumed we were the ones with the handle on it all because we *were* "like-minded."

Betty was, and still is, the example of a devoted wife, honest worker, and good person. She is smart, a brilliant musical talent, and perpetually cheery. I couldn't be around her and be blue. When I confided my inability to trust Mark (the only man on the planet she trusted was her husband), she understood me so well. I had found a soul mate. She worked full-time, so even though I couldn't hang out with her very much, we talked on the phone several times a day. She seemed to need my friendship as much as I needed hers, and that too was a great comfort.

I became very involved in the Ft. Drum government program known as The Entertainment Branch, and began fulfilling my dream of performing. I did concerts, plays, volunteered at various programs sponsored by the Entertainment Branch, and suddenly a year at Ft. Drum had gone by.

Every once in a while, I was in touch with Danny, but for some unknown reason, during the months of June, July, and August, our telephonic relationship reached a fever pitch. I was completely absorbed in listening to my mood music, and when I wasn't immersed in some play or other Entertainment Branch project, I mooned about Danny. We had begun to exchange letters more frequently. Though I believed his written words more than proved his devotion—the supposed source of my happiness—there was a part of me that was becoming aware of the recklessness of this relationship. I began to hate the element in me that was so out of control. I wanted all of this to stop; I just didn't know how. Every time he called, I asked him to make it his last. Each letter, I would write back and say it was good-bye, but one of us would break the promise. All of this fed the frenzied fantasy of this foolish and dangerous game we were playing. And it began spinning more and more out of control with each passing day.

Chapter 22

Rusty

What? Know ye not that your body is the temple of the Holy Ghost which is in you, which ye have of God, and ye are not your own? For ye are bought with a price; therefore glorify God in your body, and in your spirit, which are God's.

—1 Cor. 6:19-20 KJV

* * * * *

My secret double life was about to end. Danny was stateside for something and wanted to meet with me, but I turned him down. I cannot tell you why I did. I'm sure I could have lied my way into a trip somewhere to meet him, but for the first time, my heart didn't leap when I heard his voice. I was so bone weary of this hidden, dirty secret. At times, I felt I didn't have the strength to get up in the mornings because of the weight of it. Again, I asked him not to call me anymore. Again, I knew neither one of us would keep our promise.

The Wrong Way

Despite my stubborn refusal to forgive Mark for the things he did or didn't do, or for the things I believed he did or didn't do, it was impossible to ignore how devoted he was to me. Somewhere, deep, deep in my heart, I knew that he had changed for good, and wasn't the least bit shy about showing his genuine love and affection for me. He had been so patient with me for such a long time, and quite frankly, I didn't deserve it. Right before my eyes, in my own husband, was the man I had always dreamed of. There was simply no way to deny his dedication to our family, our marriage, and me. But I had the devil's blinders on.

It was September of 1991. My college friend's mother passed away after a long bout with cancer. Rusty had faithfully stood by me during Ross's recovery in college; now it was my turn to stand by her as her mother's disease progressed. She had been keeping me up to date on her mother's prognosis. Although her mother's condition was serious from the start, there was always hope, and Rusty held out hope until the final hours before her death. Rusty, the eldest of two brothers and a sister, was stunned and devastated when her mom quietly slipped away on a Wednesday night. She called me that night with the news.

I quickly made arrangements for Mark and the kids. I packed an overnight bag to go to her the next day, expecting to stay in a hotel so as not to cause one bit of trouble for Rusty and her family. I only knew the name of the funeral home, and a general area where it was, but I wanted to be with Rusty, and prayed the Lord would take me to her, despite the big-city traffic and the minimum eight-hour drive.

I prayed all the way south, and amazingly, the ride went well with not even one stop to use the rest room or to eat. I had to be there by 4:00 P.M. Thursday, the time of the wake. I arrived at 3:45 P.M. When I pulled into the parking lot, two extremely handsome young men were greeting people as they came into the funeral home. They wore expensive suits and identical expensive Ray-Ban sunglasses. They seemed poised and in control. The last time I had seen Rusty's brothers was in college. They were little kids then. Not any more. It was a bittersweet reunion, seeing these now-matured young men after all these years. As I hugged them, wishing I could squeeze the pain from their hearts, I asked where Rusty was. They showed me inside and for an unobserved moment, I was able to see my old, sweet, and dear friend as she accepted expressions of condolence from the guests.

Rusty came out of college with almost a perfect grade point average, and went on to be a successful business entrepreneur. She was always a beautiful, graceful, capable, savvy woman. Her elegance became more pronounced as the years passed, and despite the fact her eyes had obviously shed tears, she looked absolutely beautiful to me that sad, sad day. I knew how much her mother had meant to her and the whole family. Rusty's father died when she was a senior in high school, and her mom held the family together with love and complete devotion. Mrs. Rusticario was also greatly admired in her community.

She looked up, and this normally controlled woman ran across the room to me, threw her arms around my neck, almost falling on me, sobbing. My heart broke. I wanted to do something, anything that could ease the pain, but there was nothing to do.

She immediately asked where I was staying, and when I told her a hotel, she insisted that I stay with them. As I had driven there, I had asked God to show me what to do during my stay. This was the first funeral I would be attending as an adult, and I simply did not know what to do.

That weekend, it all fell into place. Despite the family's deep and profound grief over the loss of their beloved mother, there were times when the unity of the family brought laughter and fun into the house. All were adults with their own lives, and this albeit solemn occasion could not dampen the love that these people had for each other, and it showed.

Rusty's husband was her rock; I was so grateful she had found such a supportive, loving husband. His devotion was surely put to the test that weekend. I tried my best, and despite feeling as if I was merely in the way, Rusty, her sister, and her brothers kept telling me I was a great help and comfort. I was so grateful to God for this answered prayer. I even opened my Bible and began reading it for the first time in months.

Mrs. Rusticario was buried Saturday. It was a gorgeous sunny day, and many people turned out for the ceremony. When it was all over, and I was ready to go home, I found I didn't want to leave. This family had opened my heart with their warmth. I hadn't thought about Danny the whole weekend, and found this to be a great relief. Something happened during that weekend visit; I received so much more than I gave. It was the beginning of my road to recovering who I once was. I missed that person…the real me. The long ride home left me pensive, going over these thoughts as I headed back to all the things I was able to put aside for a time, but now had to face once again.

Chapter 23

Forty-Eight Hours

And he answering said to his father, Lo, these many years do I serve thee, neither transgressed I at any time thy commandment: and yet thou never gavest me a kid, that I might make merry with my friend: But as soon as this thy son was come, which hath devoured thy living with harlots, thou hast killed for him the fatted calf.

And he said unto him, Son, thou art ever with me, and all that I have is thine, it was meet that we should make merry, and be glad: for this thy brother was dead, and is alive again; and was lost, and is found.

—Luke 15:29-32 KJV

* * * * *

Not long after the funeral, I found myself in quite a depressed state. I had purchased a *People* magazine featuring the suicide of Joan Rivers's husband, Edgar. I sat on the living room couch reading every word, paying particular attention to *how* he took his life: alcohol and pills. Due to my migraines, I had an ample supply of Tylenol #3, or what is also known as Tylenol with codeine. There was always alcohol in our home at the time, so I began to devise a plan whereby I could end my misery the way Edgar did. The emotional pain had finally become too much. I was numb from it. I no longer had a church (although we still attended Faith Fellowship, I had not been able to feel comfortable with any church that did not teach Dr. Wierwille's dogma). I stood there in front of the bathroom mirror, the letter from the supposed love of my life in my left hand, shaking a fist at God. I was furious, I was in despair, and I felt there wasn't any hope for the happiness I had been seeking my whole life. I couldn't have the man I wanted, he was married yet I couldn't let go of him. I couldn't feel the love I should feel for my husband no matter how I tried and I couldn't measure up to the only organization that claimed it exclusively held the true teachings about God. It was ALL GOD'S FAULT. I only wanted to get to know Him. My life was falling apart, my marriage was hanging by a thread and I didn't feel I deserved to be so unhappy. I felt I deserved some kind of HAPPINESS. The pain in my life had reached such a fever pitch I was unable to stop it from spinning out of complete control and I HAD to make it stop.

"Why God? Why when all I wanted to do was know You?" I shouted at my reflection in the mirror.

I walked into the dinning room, lined up the codeine pills and got a glass for the whiskey. I then began writing the letters to my children so that when they grew up, they would know, that even though I checked out, I loved them very much.

As I began to write, I wept. I never felt so miserable and hopeless in my life. How had I let things get so far and so out of control? This was the only way out. I needed the pain to stop. There was only one thing left to do. I poured the whiskey and put a fistful of pills in my hand...

A small voice deep within me told me to call Betty. I realized I needed to say good-bye to her, so I called. She had never spoken to me in any manner other than that of tender loving care. She said these words to me in a firm, commanding tone, "Carol, you need to read the Bible. You have to stop this, and read God's Word!" Those two simple sentences made me come to my senses for some reason. I did just as she said. It was the first time I had picked up my Bible since the funeral. I began to read.

Later that day, I stood in front of our master bathroom mirror and began sobbing. I had shed many tears the last two years or so, but this time it was different. I was ready to give it all to God. I knew that even THINKING of taking my life meant that I couldn't do it by myself anymore. I reread one of Danny's most recent letters (this was *really* supposed to be our last contact), and clutching it in my hand, I fell on my face on the floor, with my arms outstretched. I begged God to help me, to come into my life and take this thing from me that had gotten so out of control. I begged him to make it stop hurting, and to take over from here because I just couldn't do it anymore.

Within forty-eight hours, Mark discovered the secret post office box and the phone card and confronted me. I almost expected it, although I had no warning. In one way, I was totally relieved. I was remarkably calm, even though he was rightfully enraged. He demanded that I stop this whole thing, and stop it NOW, or he'd walk out forever.

As he stood before me, ranting and raving, I suddenly realized that I saw him through different eyes. I could almost stand outside myself and see, for the first time in almost two years, that I didn't want to lose him. I wanted to be married to him, and I knew this with a new but solid conviction. I also knew a love for my husband that a wife should feel for the man she is married to. The Lord was working a miracle in my heart. I almost didn't hear what Mark was saying to me as these thoughts raced through my mind. I stood there as a calm washed over me, along with a peaceful knowledge of what is right.

But Mark did leave. He threw some things in a bag, and despite my unanswered calls to his office, I knew he planned to leave me for good. When it became late, I swallowed my pride, threw the kids in the car, and drove to his office. The light in his office was the only one on in the building visible from the front. I could see him sitting at his desk, grimly looking over some paperwork. I parked the car, told the kids to stay put, and went in.

We had a very heated argument. I was completely determined to make Mark come home that night. I was fighting for my life, and for the lives of our children; if he didn't come home that very night, our marriage would be damaged beyond repair. Finally, after what seemed like hours of torment, he agreed to come home.

That night was the beginning of our new marriage. I wish I could say that as swiftly as the Lord had worked a miracle in my heart, he had worked one in our marriage, but it wasn't that fast. God had some kinks to smooth in both of us, particularly me. It was a process that changed my entire life. I told Daphanie that the Lord didn't fix us; he gave us a whole new relationship.

The far-reaching consequences of the sins I had committed caused Mark a tremendous amount of pain. Even today, I am not certain he completely trusts me, despite our fantastic new relationship. As for my own opinion, it was a very long time before I was able to forgive myself. I knew that God had forgiven me, but I couldn't forgive myself. I may pay, as King David did,[20] for the rest of my life for my actions; but through the strength of Jesus Christ, I will overcome these obstacles as I serve him every day for the rest of my days.

---

[20] King David saw Bathsheba bathing and inquired after her. He found out she was the wife of a soldier, Uriah. To make Bathsheba his wife, he had Uriah killed in battle. Eventually, David repented of his sins, but for the rest of his days suffered consequences of this sin, as did many generations of his offspring. 2 Sam. 11 KJV.

Chapter 24

Harmony Returned

But put ye on the Lord Jesus Christ, and make not provision for the flesh, to fulfill the lusts thereof.

—Romans 13:14 KJV

And be not conformed to this world: but be ye transformed by the renewing of your mind, that ye may prove what is that good, and acceptable, and perfect, will of God.

—Romans 12:2 KJV

* * * * *

Another area of my life needed a miracle. When I think of it, it was the most important part of me that needed changing. I needed to be able to see The Way International for exactly what it was and is: a cult. My marriage was well on the way to being mended, but I still firmly believed that Jesus Christ was not God, and felt I would go to the grave fighting this battle against the rest of the "mistaken" Christian community. I was so blind to the fact that I worshipped the wrong god. Between Daphanie and Pastor Mike, the Lord used his servants to bring this very thing to my attention.

I began counseling with Pastor Mike just prior to the episode when I fell on my face before the throne of God, asking Jesus into my heart as my Lord. Pastor Mike became very involved with Mark and me and our relationship. It seemed odd to me that Pastor Mike wanted me to reconsider my rejection of the Trinity. I would always attempt to steer the counseling sessions away from this topic, yet Pastor Mike always managed to lead me back to this particular subject. I was puzzled because I was convinced that I was saved, that Jesus was not God, and that this was not really the crux of the matter.

His sermons at church seemed to have been prepared only for me. As I look back, it verifies how personal God can be to each of us. I'm sure there were many others who felt the Lord's personal touch on these days as well, yet I felt I was hearing a sermon designed only for me. As I sat in the pew each Sunday, I felt the Lord speaking to me. One particular Sunday, it brought me to my knees, right there in the pew, in awe and total submission. On another Sunday, Pastor preached specifically on the Trinity. That same evening, he called to express that he wasn't attempting to preach "at" me, but felt led by the Lord to speak on it. I was struck by two things: how considerate this man of God was of me when he had a huge congregation to worry about, and that although previously any sermon on that subject would have usually repelled me, this time it didn't.

Pastor continued to counsel Mark and me, but usually I went alone for my meetings with him. He would always end our time with a prayer that usually left me stunned. I became more and more impressed with this man. His patient, Christlike example was impossible to ignore. He was never judgmental, even though my lifestyle at the time gave him every right to be. He was kind, and wasn't critical, even when I confessed the sin I was continuing with Danny. I grew to respect and trust this man a great deal.

The night I dragged Mark home from the office after the discovery of my double life, I called Pastor Mike to intercede between us because the arguing was reaching a fever pitch. It was nearly 10:30 P.M., yet as Mark hollered on one extension, and I did the same on the other, he listened to us for nearly a half hour. Pastor Mike finally, but gently, interrupted us with yet again another powerful prayer over us. God worked a great miracle that night. The chains that bound me broke, because it was the first step on the long road to rediscovering the wonderful husband God had given me. Although pretty shell-shocked (Mark hadn't a clue that anything I was doing had been going on until just days prior to our altercation), he vowed to go on with our marriage, and support me if I could promise to change, and end all communication with Danny.

I was astounded to discover that I didn't *want* to communicate with Danny at all. There was such a sense of total freedom in this. I awoke the next morning without the heaviness of the guilt I had been carrying for the past two years. I truly felt like a brand-new person. It was remarkable!

I began to read my Bible again, and decided to communicate with Daphanie to tell her everything that had happened. She had been calling me, but my shame kept me from calling her. I could talk to Betty, but there had been things I just couldn't tell Daphanie. She could always see through the telephone lines, and would tell me the Lord's

Word, but I couldn't receive it until this wonderful change had taken place. I know now that no matter how mad I became when Daph called, she told me the truth and it stuck. Pastor Mike once made a powerful statement during one of his sermons that has stayed with me to this day.

"When we talk about the Lord, when we tell others about Jesus, they will believe."

He paused after this, and then repeated himself, explaining that the person might scoff, ignore us, or even become angry, but they *will believe* because it is the truth.

God's Word never comes back void, and I believe that, despite my strident rejection of my dear friend's witness, Daphanie's words got through to me because they were the truth. I harbored this truth deep in my heart, and I believe when I took the first step of making Jesus THE Lord of my life, it opened the doors to my closed heart and enabled me to reach out once again to my sweet, loving friend Daphanie. This woman had opened her home as a Christian refuge to me, despite hating the horrible sin she knew I committed and couldn't promise I wouldn't commit again. Yet she and her husband still welcomed me with love, and showed me a fine example of a family dedicated to serving Jesus Christ. It was in this home that I first discovered Christian contemporary music, which played a key role in my recovery.

It was during this time, my reunion with Daphanie, the beginning of my new marriage, and a halt to my sinful relationship with another man, that the Lord really began to perform a mighty work in me. I had stopped watching MTV entirely, and would not listen to any music, period. While I was taking a shower one day, the Lord spoke to my heart concerning music. I have found the shower to be a place where God brings thoughts to my mind through his Spirit within me. Perhaps it is because I am vulnerable or perhaps it is the water symbolism, but there is nothing standing between my soul and his voice. This simple statement came to mind: "You don't have to give up all music; why not listen to my music?"

I stood dazed as the hot water ran over me. OF COURSE! I could listen to *Christian* music! That would be safe. I came to know secular music as a very dark and evil weakness for me, as was alcohol, so I gave them both up cold turkey. I had probably listened to some form of music just about every day of my life, and missed it. Naturally, Christian music was OK!

Daphanie gave me some suggestions—my phone bill becoming quite huge in those days due to the numerous calls to my bud—and I started collecting music by Michael English, Stephen Curtis Chapman, Janet Paschall, Amy Grant, Sandi Patti, and many other contemporary Christian artists who were singing about God. In particular, Michael English spoke to my heart and ministered to me in an immense way. It was such an unparalleled joy to once again listen to music with lyrics that didn't lead to thoughts of sin. This was so uplifting! God used the incredible, powerful voice of Michael English specifically to reach into my heart—my soul—and begin the road back, as the Prodigal Son.[21] The sound of his voice, the words he sang, pierced the darkness that once surrounded my heart. I couldn't listen to a song of his, even after the tenth time, without weeping, or at the very least, getting goose bumps. By this steady musical influence, and reading the Bible, I was back, but needed healing and transformation. I certainly desired a steady stream of Christian

---

[21] The story of the Prodigal Son is found in Luke 15:11-32 KJV.

influence weaving through my life each day, because I still hadn't been able to correct a certain portion of my life yet. It was this way of thinking that needed changing the most.

I still believed Jesus was not God.

For Pastor Mike, this just wouldn't do. He and Daphanie continued to gently prod me, each in their own unique way. I swiftly became very weary of this, although my attitude honestly was: If God wants me to change this very deep-seated belief, then he'll have to show me, because I honestly do not see how it is possible that Jesus is the Son and also God. I respected Pastor Mike so much that I even tried praying to Jesus in church one day, but couldn't. I honestly believed if I did, I would be committing idolatry. I believed I could only worship God, and that although I should be grateful to his Son, I absolutely should not worship him.

But there was meekness in my heart that wasn't present before. It was at this crucial time that I believe Satan himself used one last-ditch attempt to keep my mind stayed on Wierwille's false teaching that Jesus Christ was not God. Without knowing who Jesus truly was, I couldn't become the servant that my Lord would have me be. I was driving on a country road outside Ft. Drum, New York one day when Satan manifested himself to me in my car.

Chapter 25

Revelation

In Christ alone I place my trust
And find my glory in the power of the cross
In every victory let it be said of me
My source of strength
My source of hope
Is Christ alone.

—Craig and Koch, "In Christ Alone"

* * * * *

So many cults use the trick of telling their converts to pray for a sign, or they are told there will be a demonstration of some type of supernatural manifestation to convince them that the cult and its teachings are of God. I am here to tell you this day, to believe this because it is the truth:

*SIMPLY BECAUSE ONE EXPERIENCES A SUPER-
NATURAL OCCURENCE DOES NOT MEAN IT IS
FROM GOD.*

I pray this message gets through. The Bible tells us that signs and wonders aren't always from God; it could be a trick of the devil.[22] I have previously given one example, and that was the speaking of tongues in The Way sessions. The devil can counterfeit this. Simply because this happens does not mean that God has given a sign. This next example is clearly another case of a supernatural experience that was absolutely NOT of God.

I took our little Ford Escort and went for a drive to the mall. There is a country road right outside the Fort Drum army post, and I loved the time it took, approximately fifteen minutes, because it was a pretty stretch. There were some farms and open fields. It was late fall, and the leaves were still breathtaking.

I popped in a Michael English tape and began to pray to God, thanking him for the progress Mark and I had been making. Also, due to a recent telephone conversation with Daphanie, and separately, Pastor Mike, I went before the Lord asking about the Trinity. I asked him to show me if I was wrong, because if I was, I wanted him to make it right.

---

[22] *For there shall arise false Christs, and false prophets, and shall show great signs and wonders; insomuch that, if it were possible, they shall deceive the very elect.* Matt. 24:24 KJV.

Therefore, behold, I am against the prophets, saith the Lord, that steal my words every one from his neighbour. Behold, I am against the prophets, saith the Lord, that use their tongues, and say, He saith." Jeremiah 23:30-31 KJV.

Suddenly—not shockingly, but rather directly—a large scroll appeared before me as if a huge movie screen were in front of my eyes. The scroll was rolled at first, but then it unfurled. On it was listed all the reasons that Jesus Christ was not God. This scroll probably contained at least one or two typewritten pages of information. The vision, including my reading of the inscription on the scroll, took at most five seconds. Ironically, the listed reasons were exactly what Victor Paul Wierwille had taught.

With this phenomenal occurrence, I became convinced, beyond a shadow of a doubt, that Jesus Christ was *not* God. I also realized that defending this belief would be a battle, most likely, for the rest of my life. But if it must be, it must be, because there couldn't be any doubt in my mind that this was a sign from God.

I even went so far as to tell Pastor Mike that I wouldn't discuss this subject any further. I wrote a letter to Daphanie and told her where I stood concerning the Trinity, and to accept this, or we would have to part as friends. Worn out from months of sin having taken its toll, I didn't want to battle anything else anymore. I told her she had to accept me the way I was, for whom I was, or not accept me at all.

In Daphanie's meek service to the Lord, she merely loved me back, and told me that she would indeed accept me for just exactly whom I was. I needed that at that time from her in particular. I had hardened my heart a bit, expecting her to distance herself from me (understandably so), but instead, she called with words of acceptance, love, and caring. I must admit to being a bit surprised, but grateful we did not have a confrontation. It seemed our friendship weathered yet another storm.

Although I had asked Pastor Mike to discontinue attempting to convince me that Jesus Christ *was* God—explaining that this vision had made up my mind completely, once and for all—he persisted. Shortly after I told Pastor this, he wrote me a very nice long letter, lovingly explaining why I should reconsider. It is only because of the great respect that I had for this man that I decided to humor him. I agreed I would allow him to continue our talks concerning the Trinity.

Pastor and I had several meetings where he gave me books to read (which I dutifully read, believing all along it was a complete waste of time), and then we would meet to discuss what I had read. During one of these meetings, I explained I was very willing to change my mind (and in my heart, this was true), but just couldn't see what he and Daphanie did. I really wanted to change, in a sense, because I believed Pastor when he told me how crucial this was to my recovery.

One Sunday, again, I almost felt like praying to Jesus, but had to stop short because if *they* were wrong, I'd be committing idolatry. I absolutely had to be sure they were right before I could do something like that. The vision I had, now becoming a faded, misty reminder of what I believed, began feeling wrong.

Pastor Mike also told me one day, as I tried to see the things he was telling me, that if I did change my mind, it would affect my relationship with Betty. I received this with a calm understanding. At this point in my life, I knew my relationship with God had to be settled, regardless of the fact that I may lose a friend. Betty meant a great deal to me, and I believe the Lord sent her to fill the holes in my heart temporarily while I went through my transition. She was there for me through thick and thin, but when Pastor pointed out that changing my mind could cause a rift between us, I accepted this, and merely gave it to God for him to take care of. Obviously, it was Pastor's influence as well as Daphanie's that planted seeds of God's truth.

It wasn't too much later that I sat in Faith Fellowship Church, getting ready to listen to a guest Pastor. I always preferred Pastor Mike to any other minister; however, I knew any message from the pulpit could be beneficial, so I tried to pay attention. This visiting minister began his sermon by saying that day, he would be teaching from the most misunderstood book in the Bible. He continued to talk about this book, not giving any clues as to which book he was referring to, when the thought came clear into my mind as if I were hearing an audible voice. I suddenly knew that the book he referred to was the book of Revelation. I also knew I needed to turn to that book immediately.

I am not one who puts much store in opening a page of the Bible randomly and automatically assuming God is trying to give me a message through the pages. Yet the first page I opened to was the beginning of Revelation: *I am Alpha and Omega, the first and the last...*[23]

It was as if that proverbial light had turned on in my brain. Could it be? I went back to the beginning of chapter one, and read the whole chapter, in context. Then I happened to turn to another section:

> *And I saw a new heaven and a new earth: for the first heaven and the first earth were passed away; and there was no more sea. And I John saw the holy city, new Jerusalem, coming down from God out of heaven, prepared as a*

---

[23] Revelation 1:11 KJV

bride adorned for her husband. And I heard a great voice out of heaven saying, Behold, the tabernacle of God is with men, and he will dwell with them, and they shall be his people, and God himself shall be with them, and be their God. And God shall wipe away all tears from their eyes; and there shall be no more death, neither sorrow, nor crying, neither shall there be any more pain: for the former things are passed away. And he that sat upon the throne said, Behold, I make all things new. And he said unto me, Write: for these words are true and faithful. And he said unto me, It is done. I am Alpha and Omega, the beginning and the end. I will give unto him that is athirst of the fountain of the water of life freely. He that overcometh shall inherit all things; and I will be his God, and he shall be my son. But the fearful, and unbelieving, and the abominable, and murderers, and whoremongers, and sorcerers, and idolaters, and all liars, shall have their part in the lake which burneth with fire and brimstone: which is the second death.[24]

It hit me like a sledgehammer. Jesus Christ WAS God!

There was no doubt that in chapter 1, John saw Christ, who stated that he is the Alpha and the Omega! Only God is the

---

[24] Revelation 21:1-8 KJV

first and the last, as he said in Isaiah![25] Again, in chapter 21, those verses speak of our God, our Christ, sitting on his mighty throne. In verse 6, he says he is the Alpha and the Omega. Pastor was right! Daph was right! They all were, and I had been so very wrong! I also knew at that very moment that Daphanie was right about other things. I had been loyal all this time to a cult.

That very day, my life took an even more dramatic turn. I knew that I had to keep this newfound insight from Betty, and other Way friends I was still very much in contact with. I began to explore this Jesus, the man, my God, my Savior, whom I had never really known for all those years of my life.

On that day, I was delivered from the teachings of The Way International. It was the beginning of an absolutely new way of reading the Bible. Portions I had never read, because The Way taught that only the Gospels were for Wayers; while we could learn from the rest, the Gospels contained the scriptures we should study and concentrate on. It was as if I began reading the Bible for the first time. The same scriptures I had read over and over for years now took on a new meaning. Jesus was Lord and he was my God!

Because of the lies The Way taught, in particular pertaining to the deity of Christ, I believed in a different god. It was because of this that I knew my life had been terribly incomplete. I had been denied a close, personal relationship with my Jesus, the very Lord who has become the entire center of my being. I remember a tune I once heard that

---

[25] *Who hath wrought and done it, calling the generations from the beginning? I the Lord, the first, and with the last; I am he. Isa. 41:4 KJV.*
Hearken unto me, O Jacob and Israel, my called; I am he; I am the first, I also am the last. Isa. 48:12 KJV.

soothed, "I can't even walk without holding his hand." I can't walk without Jesus. For all those long years, I had been trying to live my whole life merely by referring to him in a crisis. When in The Way, though I thought I had developed a right relationship with Jesus Christ, I still didn't know him. I never had, until he came into my life and made me whole. Through it all, on my long journey back from a cult, I found Jesus. And it was Jesus who delivered me from my insecurities. I was delivered from my need to seek humans or human organizations in order to feel peace. I received a peace that surpasses ALL understanding the day I realized who Jesus WAS, who he IS, and who he has yet to be in my life!

I WAS SET FREE!

> *And he said unto him, Son, thou art ever with me, and all that I have is thine. It was meet that we should make merry, and be glad: for this thy brother was dead, and is alive again; and was lost, and is found.*[26]

---

26 Luke 15:31-32 KJV

Chapter 26

Answering "Why?"

Not every one that saith unto me, Lord, Lord, shall enter into the kingdom of heaven; but he that doeth the will of my Father which is in heaven. Many will say to me in that day, Lord, Lord, have we not prophesied in thy name? and in thy name have cast out devils? and in thy name done many wonderful works? And then will I profess unto them, I never knew you: depart from me, ye that work iniquity. Therefore whosoever heareth these sayings of mine, and doeth them, I will liken him unto a wise man, which built his house upon a rock: And the rain descended, and the floods came, and the winds blew, and beat upon that house; and it fell not: for it was founded upon a rock. And every one that heareth these sayings of mine, and doeth them not, shall be likened unto a foolish man, which built his house upon the sand: And the rain descended, and the floods came, and the winds blew, and beat upon that house; and it fell: and great was the fall of it. And it came to pass, when Jesus had ended these sayings, the people were astonished at his doctrine: For he taught them as one having authority, and not as the scribes.

—Matt. 7:21-29 KJV

The Wrong Way

And when he was come out of the ship, immediately there met him out of the tombs a man with an unclean spirit, Who had his dwelling among the tombs; and no man could bind him, no, not with chains: Because that he had been often bound with fetters and chains, and the chains had been plucked asunder by him, and the fetters broken in pieces: neither could any man tame him. And always, night and day, he was in the mountains, and in the tombs, crying, and cutting himself with stones. But when he saw Jesus afar off, he ran and worshipped him, And cried with a loud voice, and said, What have I to do with thee, Jesus, thou Son of the most high God? I adjure thee by God, that thou torment me not. For he said unto him, Come out of the man, thou unclean spirit. And he asked him, What is thy name? And he answered, saying, My name is Legion: for we are many.

—Mark 5:2-9 KJV

* * * * *

I would like to say that with my deliverance came a perfected life. This is not the case. The Lord took his time in showing me the things I needed to change in my life in order to better serve him. I am still changing and growing with each day, as the Lord takes the old Carol and brings in more of Jesus. One thing he did was answer my question, "Why?"

My merciful God did not have to answer at all. I was willing to serve him even if I never knew the answer to that question. Soon after I realized that The Way teachings were from the perspective of a brainwashing cult, the Lord gave me two scriptures that opened my eyes as they had never been opened before.

It is not enough to know who Jesus is. Demons know him. In Luke 8:26-34, when Jesus arrived at Gadarenes, a Gentile town, he was confronted by a man who long had demons within him.

> *When this man saw Jesus, he cried out, and fell down before him, and with a loud voice said, What have I to do with thee Jesus, thou Son of God most high? I beseech thee, torment me not.* [27]

These demons that had plagued this man knew just exactly who Jesus was. Just as I had known who Jesus was for most of my life. I knew who he was, but I didn't really KNOW him.

In addition, there is a danger of profession without faith, and in his own words, Jesus tells us what that is in Matthew 7:21-29. Paying particular attention here to verses 21-23:

> *Not every one that saith unto me, Lord, Lord, shall enter into the kingdom of heaven; but he that doeth the will of my Father which is in heaven. Many will say to me in that day, Lord, Lord, have we not prophesied in thy name? and in thy name have cast out devils? and in thy name done many wonderful works? And then will I profess unto them, I never knew you: depart from me, ye that work iniquity.* [28]

---

[27] Luke 8:28 KJV
[28] Matthew 7:21-23 KJV

Many people say to me, "I have an honest heart, I obey God's commandments, I'm generous to the poor, I don't believe for one moment that God is that horrible that I would be condemned to eternal hell when I honestly have a heart to know him. God knows my heart."

God knows your heart, but if, as it is in the case of cult members, you worship another god, then he cannot honor what is in your heart. Good intentions don't a salvation make. It isn't by simply THINKING we know who he is because we have a subjective, supernatural experience, or by being a good person that we can be saved. It isn't even studying his Word, the Bible, as I did for six years while I was a cult member, that will save us. We must first worship the correct God; we must know the one and ONLY true God and worship him in TRUTH, asking forgiveness for our sins:

> *That if thou shalt confess with thy mouth the Lord Jesus, and shalt believe in thine heart that God hath raised him from the dead, thou shalt be saved. For with the heart man believeth unto righteousness; and with the mouth confession is made unto salvation. For the scripture saith, Whosoever believeth on him shall not be ashamed* [29]

> *God is a Spirit: and they that worship him must worship him in spirit and in truth.* [30]

---

[29] Romans 10:9-11 KJV
[30] John 4:24 KJV

> *Jesus saith unto him, I am the way, the truth,*
> *and the life: no man cometh unto the Father,*
> *but by me.[31]*

The next step is to profess our complete commitment to him, which includes a life-changing experience and study of his Word. You must make him Lord of your life, not just Lord IN your life. Many call it being born again of God's Spirit:

> *Jesus answered and said unto him, Verily,*
> *verily, I say unto thee, Except a man be born*
> *again, he cannot see the kingdom of God.*
> *Nicodemus saith unto him, How can a man be*
> *born when he is old? can he enter the second*
> *time into his mother's womb, and be born?*
> *Jesus answered, Verily, verily, I say unto thee,*
> *Except a man be born of water and of the*
> *Spirit, he cannot enter into the kingdom of*
> *God. That which is born of the flesh is flesh;*
> *and that which is born of the Spirit is spirit.*
> *Marvel not that I said unto thee, Ye must be*
> *born again. The wind bloweth where it listeth,*
> *and thou hearest the sound thereof, but canst*
> *not tell whence it cometh, and whither it*
> *goeth: so is every one that is born of the*
> *Spirit. [32]*

> *Being born again, not of corruptible seed, but*
> *of incorruptible, by the word of God, which*

---

[31] John 14:6 KJV
[32] John 3:3-8 KJV

liveth and abideth forever. For all flesh is as grass, and all the glory of man as the flower of grass. The grass withereth, and the flower thereof falleth away: But the word of the Lord endureth for ever. And this is the word which by the gospel is preached unto you. [33]

The final step is to cultivate a desire to learn God's Word:

Wherefore laying aside all malice, and all guile, and hypocrisies, and envies, and all evil speakings, As newborn babes, desire the sincere milk of the word, that ye may grow thereby: If so be ye have tasted that the Lord is gracious. [34]

I beseech you therefore, brethren, by the mercies of God, that ye present your bodies a living sacrifice, holy, acceptable unto God, which is your reasonable service. And be not conformed to this world: but be ye transformed by the renewing of your mind, that ye may prove what is that good, and acceptable, and perfect, will of God. [35]

This is not to claim that I know who is or who is not saved. This is between the person and God. I am telling you what God showed me, in answer to my heartfelt question, "Why?"

Why did this happen to me?

---

[33] 1 Peter 1:23-25 KJV
[34] 1 Peter 2:1-3 KJV
[35] Romans 12:1-2 KJV

The other thing he was so kind to show me in a very personal way was that despite my sins, despite the terrible things I had done and the harm I inflicted on my family and marriage, I am WORTHY of his love. I am his beloved child, and forgiveness is complete when we are born again of his Spirit. Can I still sin? Of course I can, but my past is in the past, and I need not dwell on it. This was a process that took over two years for me to fully comprehend. The shame of having been duped into belonging to a cult haunted me as well as the sin of what I had done subsequent to leaving the cult. I began working so hard in my service to the Lord I was exhausting myself. I would stay up through the night, posting on Internet bulletin boards, warning about The Way and other cults. A virtual stranger, someone who had been reading my messages on these boards, sent me an e-mail asking, "Do you ever sleep?"

I wrote back some trite thing, appreciating her concern but essentially dismissing her. Despite my children complaining and my husband and friends gently warning me, I was obsessing. How can one obsess about GOD, would be my reply! But one can.

I wasn't listening to what God wanted me to do, I was doing what I thought I had to do to come to a place where I could forgive myself and actually BELIEVE God forgave me. Silly me. Nothing I could ever do could make me worthy. Jesus did that for me on Calvary. He washed me clean, and took my sins away, no matter how grievous. No one can work his or her way into grace. It is a gift freely given by God through his Son Jesus Christ. Grace is FREE, utterly and completely FREE. It is by his grace we are saved, not our works.[36]

Then my Jesus lovingly gave me these words through this stranger I met on the Internet:

> *Hold on, be not discouraged My precious and faithful one, for good things are on the way. Many prayers shall I answer but in My timing. You have labored before Me and it has not been in vain. Be not weary in well-doing for you shall reap. Rest, dear one. Rest. Rest in Me. All is well. You do not have to prove anything to Me. Rest. Rest. Rest. For your soul is weary and your spirit in need of refreshing. Lean on My everlasting arms which shall never fail you. I love you.*

As I reread those words, I still get the chills.

It took me a long time to come to terms with the why of my trial. Then I began to realize, through the Lord Jesus Christ, I am who I am today because of my past. I had been beating myself over the head for taking so long to figure it all out! I was humiliated that I was so blinded and had been too prideful to realize that what I had been looking for all my life was always there. Jesus was right beside me all along, but I tried running the race on my own. I thought it was by my personal strength that I could accomplish great things in this life, without Jesus, even when my heart was to do these things *for* my Heavenly Father. I can do nothing. I just had to learn

---

[36] *For by grace are ye saved through faith; and that not of yourselves: it is the gift of God: Not of works, lest any man should boast.* Eph. 2:8-9 KJV.

that I can't do it without him, I can't even walk without holding his hand, and once I knew this, my life came together.

I also discovered that I really am forgiven. I believed that God could forgive me—or I tried my best to understand this—but I definitely couldn't forgive myself. Deep down, I couldn't understand how God could. It was a process before I was able to believe both.

My Father forgave me, and tossed it all in the sea of forgetfulness. I am forever grateful to my God, my wonderful Jesus, for his love and forgiveness. There is no other feeling on this earth that can compare to that comforting knowledge. Peace, he brings me peace, and it is unshakable, despite the trials and tribulations we Christians face in life. Now, for the rest of the days of my life, I will tell others about him.

Epilogue

While I would like to report all is well with all souls, I cannot. Sadly, in researching this book, I called our first Twig leaders in L.A. They said they have seen "Bill" frequently, and the terrible account is that he has been spotted at the entrance to a certain L.A. freeway, begging for money. He seems to have sunk deeper into insanity, and his drug dependence is what fuels his existence. Darlene has since remarried.

I tried to continue a relationship with Betty, but she stopped speaking to me due to my outspoken stand against The Way. A few years ago, quite by surprise, she contacted me by e-mail. We began a back-and-forth correspondence, which eventually led to her asking me about Jesus Christ, the one *not* taught by The Way. I sent her a rough copy of this book, told her what I came to know, and I believe today she knows the truth of the Savior she has always endeavored to serve!

I am very blessed to share about my mother. What started as terrible news has ended in a victory for our Lord and God.

The Wrong Way

In November 1995, my wonderful stepfather was diagnosed with terminal cancer. Both my atheist mother and stepfather came to know the Lord Jesus Christ as they struggled through this fight. Although the battle ended in the death of my stepfather's body, I believe he will have eternal life. Jesus conquered death on the cross. Praise him! So, although my stepfather's body will no longer be useful here on earth, his heart and soul will live forever with Jesus as we all await his imminent return.

Recently, my husband and I celebrated our twenty-third anniversary. Amazing! Shortly after my exit from The Way and my release from the brainwashing my mind had been in such bondage to, we renewed our wedding vows. I shudder to think that I almost destroyed what God had truly put together. My husband is without a doubt a perfect soul mate, handpicked by my Father in heaven to be my companion for life. I don't say this lightly, but Mark is truly the love of my life. Jesus *is* my life, and he gave me life so that I could grow old with the man who is the love of my life. God is so good!

Remember that God cares for you. Yes, you! It doesn't matter what you've done, or what you think is unforgivable. There is nothing God can't or won't forgive. He saved a wretch like me; he can save you too. You have to allow him in, though. You must let him have your heart. It's easy…just a small step, a simple leap of faith. Just tell him you want him in your life, and as Romans 10:9-10 tells us, when you confess your sins, confess that Jesus Christ is Lord and was raised from the dead, and believe this in your heart, you are saved. PIECE OF CAKE! Don't wait one more moment or another day. Now is the time! Do it today! You'll never regret it!

Epilogue

If you have wandered down a path away from him, if you need to renew your strength and you are weary of the ways this world draws us in and eats away at the very fiber of our soul, then come back to him. You can't even imagine a sin that God can't forgive. He wants you to come home. Come back to the open arms that long to embrace you, let him take control of all of your suffering. Allow him to take care of you. Let go of this world and your pain and hurts, let go and let God! He's waiting for you because he loves you! Don't be ashamed; don't hesitate because you feel you aren't worthy. You are worthy because the blood of the Lamb covers your sin! Make him Lord of your life; there is no better time than RIGHT NOW.

Seek him while you can; our redemption draweth nigh!

Carol J. Van Drie
"In Christ alone I place my trust…"

October 2002

Just What Is a Cult Anyway?

The word "cult" is heavily charged with negative connotations. As a result, many people resist having their group or faith institution labeled with this term. So, what is a cult? What do the experts say?

In her book *Cults in Our Midst: The Hidden Menace in Our Everyday Lives,* Dr. Margaret Singer gives some distinct guidelines we can use to begin our discussion on what is or is not a cult. Singer lists three key factors that contribute to a group being labeled a cult:

1. The origin of the group and role of the leader
2. The power structure or the relationship between the leader (or leaders) and the followers
3. The use of a coordinated program of persuasion (which is called thought reform or, more commonly, brainwashing)[37]

---

[37]Margaret Singer, *Cults in Our Midst: The Hidden Menace in Our Everyday Lives* (San Francisco: Jossey-Bass, 1995), p. 7.

Singer clearly indicates that what one researcher may call a cult, another may not. Therefore, further definition is required because not all cults are alike. There are religious cults, political cults, business cults, and so on. For this discussion, we will mainly concentrate on religious or Christian cults.

Singer elaborates on the definition of a cult by adding the following three principles:

1. Cults are established by strong or charismatic leaders who control power hierarchies and material resources

2. Cults possess some revealed "word" in the form of a book, manifesto, or doctrine

3. Cults create fortified boundaries, confining their membership in various ways and attacking those who would leave as defectors, deserters, or traitors; they recruit new members with ruthless energy and raise enormous sums of money; and they tend to view the outside world with increasing hostility and distrust as the organization ossifies[38]

The Reverend Richard L. Dowhower, author of several well-known cult recovery books, also provides an outline of the characteristics of cults:

A. They practice intentionally fraudulent and deceptive recruitment and fund-raising. Their official ethic of "holy deception" justifies intentional lying. These practices deny persons the right of informed consent.

---

[38] Ibid., p. 39.

For example, if you ask a Mormon missionary if he or she believes in the Trinity, the answer will be yes. However, this affirmation is based on the LDS (Latter-day Saints) Articles of Faith, which state, "We believe in God, the Eternal Father, and in His Son, Jesus Christ, and in the Holy Ghost." Therefore, unless you know the history behind the Articles of Faith, you will not be aware that this statement is misleading. What the LDS missionary will not tell you—and may not even be aware of—is that Mormons believe that God the Father (Elohim) is one god, Jesus (Jehovah) is another god, and the Holy Ghost is yet another god. Just as they most likely will not elaborate on their believing in the three gods of the Trinity, they will neglect to mention their belief that all good Mormons who participate in the Mormon Temple Ceremony rites and who follow Mormon dogma perfectly can themselves turn into gods and goddesses someday.

B. The most destructive of their unethical and manipulative practices is mind control: a purposeful practice of inducing a form of involuntary servitude, also known as thought reform, brainwashing, and coercive persuasion. Such practices of "undue influence" violate our civil laws.

Characteristics are:

- Denigration of independent analytical and critical thinking
- Induction of anxiety, fear, and guilt, which can be relieved only by conformity to the group
- Selective group reinforcement and punishment of the member's actions, attitudes, and beliefs

- Deliberate control of information in order to limit alternatives from which members may choose
- Promising to relieve members' sense of inadequacy by claiming exalted powers for the group and its leader
- Induction of dissociative thinking and trancelike states (sometimes through a physically debilitating diet and regimen), which narrow attention, induce specious insights, and impair judgment

C. Financial exploitation of members, their families, and the public at large becomes a form of religious racketeering in which the cult refuses to be held accountable to the public from which it raises funds.

It has been my experience that most cults—including Mormonism, The Way, and Scientology—place a huge emphasis on giving money. In Mormonism, for example, a person must *pay* to go to Mormon heaven. If a member does not tithe (give 10 percent of his or her income), then he or she cannot participate in the Mormon Temple Ceremony. If a Mormon does not participate in the Temple Ceremony (sealing himself or herself to a Mormon spouse), he or she cannot go to Mormon heaven.[39] Thus, no pay, no heaven.[40]

---

[39] Secret ceremonies, also known as "Temple Work," are performed in the Mormon Temple. The most important ceremonies are Baptism for the Dead and Temple Marriage. As two experts on Mormonism state, "Mormon leaders teach that the spirits of people who have died cannot enter the kingdom of heaven until a Mormon is baptized for them by

proxy." Jerald and Sandra Tanner, *Mormonism: Shadow or Reality?* (Salt Lake City: Utah Lighthouse Ministry, 1987), p. 451.

The Temple Marriage is explained as follows: "The Mormon Church teaches that it is necessary for a person to be married or sealed in the Temple so that he can obtain the highest exaltation in the hereafter. This work is done for both the living and the dead. The doctrine of Temple Marriage comes from Section 132 of the Doctrine and Covenants. This is a revelation given to Joseph Smith on July 12, 1843." Ibid., p. 455.

Quoting the Doctrine and Covenants directly: "And again, verily I say unto you, if a man marry a wife by my word, which is my law, and by the new and everlasting covenant, and it is sealed unto them by the Holy Spirit of promise, by him who is anointed, unto whom I have appointed this power and the keys of this priesthood; and it shall be; it shall be said unto them—Ye shall come forth in the first resurrection; and if it be after the first resurrection, in the next resurrection; and shall inherit thrones, kingdoms, principalities, and powers, dominions, all heights and depths...Then shall they be gods, because they have no end; therefore shall they be from everlasting to everlasting, because they continue; then shall they be above all, because all things are subject unto them. Then shall they be gods, because they have all power, and the angels are subject unto them. Verily, verily, I say unto you, except ye abide my law ye cannot attain to this glory." Doctrine and Covenants, Section 132, verses 19–20.

40 "We have said pay your Tithing, And we have said to the Bishops that if any man refuses to pay his Tithing, try him for his fellowship; and if he still refuses, cut him off from the Church..." *Journal of Discourses*, Vol. 10, pp. 283 and 285.

Also, a Latter-day Saints teachers' manual states: "Those seeking recommends should be faithfully attending sacrament meetings, priesthood meetings, and other Church meetings. They should be conscientiously carrying out their callings given through priesthood authority. They should be striving to keep all of the Lord's commandments, including paying a full tithe..." *Endowed from on High: Temple Preparation Seminar Teacher's Manual* (Salt Lake City,

The Way International places a tremendous amount of pressure on members to not only tithe, but to give "abundant sharing" above and beyond tithing. Those who don't are usually considered out of fellowship.

D.   Physical abuse and even death occur to animals and humans. Especially prevalent is physical and sexual abuse of women and children.

This abhorrent behavior is rampant in numerous cults: Jim Jones of the People's Temple, the Branch Davidians, The Way, and Mormonism[41] are just a few of these groups that sexually exploited/exploit their most vulnerable members.

E.   Because most groups have a grandiose scheme of world leadership and predict imminent apocalypse—the end of the world—they represent a threat to democratic political systems, and, in the military, to command authority.

The Jehovah's Witnesses believe that all of Christendom and the world's cultures are evil. Therefore adherence to any government entity is forbidden. Witnesses are not allowed to pledge allegiance to the flag, vote, or serve in the U.S. military.

Rev. Dowhower points out that there are those who would become offended by "cultic truth claims." However, I am in complete agreement with Rev. Dowhower as to

---

Utah: Church of Jesus Christ of Latter-day Saints, 1995), p. 9.
[41] Jerald and Sandra Tanner, "Mormonism's Problem with Child Sexual Abuse," *Salt Lake City Messenger*, no. 91 (November 1996). See also Rick Branch, "Mormonism and the Family: How Much Is That Family in the Window?" *Watchman Expositor* 6, no. 10 (1989).

these other elements that identify Christian cult characteristics in particular. Rev. Dowhower uses the following criteria as a general guideline to cult characteristics; however, I find his listing especially pertinent when discussing Christian cults. Cults violate the Christian tradition by denying:

1. the validity of Jesus as savior,
2. the sufficiency of the Holy Bible as revelation, and
3. the adequacy of the fellowship of traditional churches. Their "salvation by special enlightenment" is a revisiting of the ancient Gnostic heresy. Some actually promise to make the believers into gods.

In addition, there are modern Christian-cult criteria, which I call "red flags," that should alert anyone interested in a group that embodies these characteristics. The individual should take a long hard look at any religious organization that would answer yes to any of the following questions. They echo Rev. Dowhower's list above, with a few additions:

Red Flag #1: Is the organization anti-Trinity? Is there a denial of the very basic Orthodox historical Christian teaching that Jesus Christ is God who came to earth in the flesh?[42] Is there an attempt to make Jesus a separate entity altogether from God? Is the group anti-Catholic? Anti-Jew?

---

[42] "Doctrine of the Trinity. The central dogma of Christian Theology. Viz. that the One God exists in Three Persons and One Substance...The Trinitarian teaching thus elaborated by the Scholastics, though challenged in the 17th cent. by Socinianism and Unitarianism, has

Red Flag #2: Will the organization disclose to its members all of its earnings and donations and what it does with these monies?

Red Flag #3: Does the group have another "holy" book or other divinely "inspired" works that it relies heavily upon? Does the group make claims that there was a need to have this newly inspired addition to Holy Scripture because the Bible is incomplete, missing parts, and/or incorrectly translated?

Red Flag #4: Does the religious organization have a leader (usually but not always male) or founder who is considered a "prophet" or "teacher" or "seer" or has any association with this type of description? Does this leader have the only true teachings from God? Was this "revelation" considered to be new and given to this leader, and this leader alone?

Red Flag #5: Does the group consider all or most all other Christian organizations to be "fallen" or "corrupt" or even evil, lacking the real truths about the Bible and God, while making claims that its particular organization is the only group that possesses godly and biblical truths?

Red Flag #6: Do the members of the group tend to approach you and others with a focus on what is wrong with other churches' teachings, or on their church or

---

remained the common inheritance of subsequent W. Theology." *The Oxford Dictionary of the Christian Church*, 3rd ed.

organization and its exclusive knowledge of the things of God, rather than talking about Jesus Christ?

Red Flag #7: Do the members of this group tend to use the name of Jesus far, far less (if ever) than they use the word "God"? In other words, is the emphasis upon worship of God as the Father as opposed to Jesus Christ the Savior?

Just because one of these red flags pops up does not mean the group is a cult. However, if denial of the Trinity is one basis of the teachings of any group that attempts to call itself Christian, the organization may not be a cult, but it shouldn't be calling itself Christian. Therefore, you should avoid this deception.

One exception to the second red flag would be the Catholic Church. Traditionally, the Catholic Church has not revealed its holdings to its membership. However, the Catholic Church adheres to traditional Orthodox Christian beliefs such as the Trinity and the Bible being the holy, inerrant word of God. In the case of the Mormon Church (or, as it is also called, the Church of Jesus Christ of Latter-day Saints), the net worth of the church and what it does with its members' mandatory tithing is never revealed and is kept quite secret from members. In cases like this, that red flag is a serious caution against becoming involved with an organization that refuses to reveal what it does with the money of its membership. What is it that the organization has to hide? Why won't it reveal what is done with its members' money?

Use of the term "cult" is fair when it is applied to churches or religious organizations that meet the criteria that have been discussed here, even if the groups named don't agree. Generally, those who object to any usage of this term are members of cults themselves. Primarily because there seems to be false association with the most destructive cults, objections are raised to using the term at all. All cults are destructive, but not all cults will result in their members drinking poisoned Kool-Aid or burning to death in a compound. Nonetheless, all cults are destructive in some manner, either psychologically or physically, or, in most cases, both.

Further supporting the defining characteristics of a cult, John Ankerberg and John Weldon, in their book *Encyclopedia of Cults and New Religions*, point out:

> Despite the claim to be Christian or to be compatible with Christianity, there is a misrepresentation of Christianity, such as the distortion of the Christian gospel and Christian theology, and, further, an insulation against the gospel with pervasive unbiblical theology generally. For example, the two most vital biblical doctrines are universally rejected. First, there is denial of the Holy Trinity: God, Jesus Christ and the Holy Spirit. Second, despite a claim to teach salvation by grace, salvation by effort and character is universal and pervasive, often logically connected to devaluation or rejection of the atonement. And in many groups, there is a hostility to Christianity once you get past the outer friendly face.[43]

---

[43] John Ankerberg and John Weldon, *Encyclopedia of Cults and New*

There are groups today that not only demand to be called Christian, but also claim to be the only true Christian organization. Groups such as The Way, Mormonism, and Jehovah's Witnesses boldly make this claim, yet their teachings are not Christian and deny the very basic, fundamental principles historical Orthodox Christianity has been based on for more than two thousand years. These organizations that came along nearly two thousand years after Christianity would have us believe that they suddenly possess truths kept secret from Christians and only revealed to their own founder, prophet, or teacher. These groups misrepresent themselves and Christianity and cultivate anti-Catholicism, anti-Semitism and, in general, anti-Christianity.

On page XXIII of the encyclopedia, Ankerberg and Weldon explain that regardless of the claims these groups make regarding freedom of self-expression, if a member attempts to question or disagree with anything within the organizational leadership, the individual may not only be punished, but excommunicated.

Members are also pressured into disassociating themselves from family members or spouses who do not belong to their organization. I know of several members of the Mormon Church who had spouses who decided to leave the church; these members were then pressured to divorce their non-Mormon spouses.[44] In one case, a woman's new

---

Religions (Eugene, Ore.: Harvest House, 1999), p. XXIII.

[44] Without marriage to another Mormon, the highest Mormon heaven is unattainable. See *Mormonism: Shadow or Reality?* p. 455: "The

Mormon boyfriend was reported to authorities as well as to the school principal because the children were being abused; however, the authorities turned a blind eye because they themselves were Mormon. In the state of South Carolina where this happened, it is the law that any school authority must report suspected child abuse (the abuses were reported by older siblings who were eyewitnesses), yet the law was defied because those who heard the reports were themselves Mormon. When the former Mormon asked his ex-wife if they could consider reconciliation (a move to try to protect his children), she confessed that she had to marry this abusive man because she had to try to get to heaven. She told him reconciliation would be impossible.[45]

Cult members must work themselves into heaven.

As Boyd K. Packer, acting president of the Quorum of the Twelve Apostles, stated in an address at Brigham Young University in February 1998, "We are not saved by grace alone."[46]

Mormon Church teaches that it is necessary for a person to be married or sealed in the Temple so that he can obtain the highest exaltation in the hereafter…The doctrine of Temple Marriage comes from Section 132 of the Doctrine and Covenants. This is revelation given to Joseph Smith on July 12, 1843. Joseph Fielding Smith, the tenth President of the Church, made these statements: 'If you want salvation in the *fullest*, that is *exaltation* in the kingdom of God, so that you may become his sons and daughters, you have got to go into the *temple* of the Lord and receive these holy ordinances which belong to that house, which cannot be had elsewhere.' (*Doctrines of Salvation*, Vol. 2, p. 44)"

[45] A former Mormon, interviews by the author, April 2000.

[46] *Encyclopedia of Cults and New Religions*, p. 301.

Much like Mormons, Jehovah's Witnesses stress that while works based on the Old Testament do not attain salvation, it is works taught in the New Testament that will save a soul.[47] Orthodox historical Christianity teaches that we are saved by grace and grace alone.[48]

Ankerberg and Weldon explain that these groups claim to interpret the Bible properly, but they continue to systematically misinterpret the Bible by using additional materials or additional revelation or through other means that distort biblical truths.[49]

Again, as indicated in the Ankerberg/Weldon criteria, there can be no independent thinking within these cults. For years Wayers were strongly discouraged from getting computers and surfing the Internet. Scientology literally pursues with threats and anonymous harassment anyone who would go public with information the organization does not wish made public. When Mormons leave the church, they often will receive anonymous threatening calls in an attempt to either threaten them back into Mormonism or shut them up.[50] I interviewed a former Mormon, "Luke," at the height of his ordeal. When Luke left the church, his Mormon wife was pressured into leaving him. He went public with a document revealing the Mormon Church's attempts to interfere with his visitation rights with his

---

[47] Ibid., p. 153.

[48] Eph. 2:7–9: That in the ages to come he might show the exceeding riches of his grace in his kindness toward us through Christ Jesus. For by grace are ye saved through faith; and that not of yourselves: it is the gift of God: Not of works, lest any man should boast.

[49] *Encyclopedia of Cults and New Religions*, p. XXIII.

[50] A former Mormon, interviews by the author, April 2000.

children. Luke told me he began receiving anonymous calls, threatening that he would never see his children again if he didn't stop going public with his accusations. He also revealed that the Mormon leadership was well aware that these types of anonymous threats were made as a regular course of action against those who would leave the church. He knew because this was something *he* had done for the Mormon Church for years with the full knowledge of the highest-ranking Mormon leadership. Luke made these calls from official church buildings with the leadership's full support and permission. (This was before caller ID was widely used). He knew that the threats of never seeing his children were valid, as there is a vast underground network, also sanctioned by the LDS Church, that will take the family members and hide them while bankrolling any litigation for the family against any non-Mormon taking legal action in divorce cases.[51]

Cults will claim that they give their members true spirituality and a genuine experience of God and do not have occult practices.[52] The secret Mormon Temple Ceremony is a perfect example of an extreme occult practice in part based on a nonreligious Masonic temple ceremony.[53] Cults will also claim that they accurately present their organization's history.[54] However, the history of the leader and the organization will often be distorted and manipulated. Cults not only often practice dishonesty,

---

[51] A former Mormon, interviews by the author, April 2000.

[52] *Encyclopedia of Cults and New Religions*, p. XXIV.

[53] *Mormonism: Shadow or Reality?* p. 484.

[54] *Encyclopedia of Cults and New Religions*, p. XXIV.

but they will encourage it. Cult organizations will also claim to be open, but often they are extremely secretive and will even practice secret ceremonies. The Mormon Church not only disallows anyone who is not a "worthy" Mormon to participate in the Temple Ceremony, but it forbids the discussion of this ceremony in any manner by its own members.

While the term "cult" generally brings to mind radical groups such as Jim Jones's the People's Temple or David Koresh's group, the Branch Davidians, I have learned in my decade-long study of cult groups, in particular Christian cults, that this term can be fairly applied to other groups such as the Jehovah's Witnesses, the Mormons, or others that meet the criteria discussed above.

Any group can be a cult or even become a cult. Jim Jones's Temple "opened up a pet shelter, three convalescent centers, a forty-acre home for boys. Many in the congregation had taken foster children into their care. All of these activities reflected well on the church in the eyes of the [Redwood Valley, Calif.] community."[55] While there was an underbelly of evil that always seemed to exist from the inception of the People's Temple, in the beginning this group was very beneficial to the surrounding community.

Interestingly, the Worldwide Church of God appears to be the only cult that has ever completely transformed itself from cult status to a mainstream Christian denomination. The organization's Web site is very open about the past

---

[55] Minn Yee, *In My Father's House: The Story of the Layton Family and the Reverend Jim Jones* (New York: Berkley Books, 1982, p. 110).

nonbiblical teachings of the group's founder. Today, the organization has dropped these nonbiblical teachings and now is "in full agreement with the statement of faith of the National Association of Evangelicals."[56]

The Worldwide Church of God is a good example of a cult recognizing its nonbiblical practices and correcting its ways. Unfortunately, the same cannot be said of other groups discussed here.

This document is not a comprehensive list of all cults or suspected cults. This material was prepared to help those of you who are not sure what a cult might be. Use the criteria presented here to judge a religious organization you aren't familiar with before becoming involved. Any legitimate organization can *turn into* a cult. Some organizations, such as The Way, the Jehovah's Witnesses, and the Mormon Church, started as cults and remain so to this day.

Be wary and be careful. My suggestion is do not enter any new church or religious organization without researching it. Watch for the red flags listed here, and ask questions. If a red flag pops up, the organization may not be a cult, but before making any commitment to the group or attending services or meetings, research that red flag further. Be wise about your place of worship; it could affect your life for the better—or, if it's a cult—for the worse.

---

[56] "Transformed by Christ: A Brief History of the Worldwide Church of God." Retrieved October 29, 2003, from http://www.wcg.org/lit/AboutUs/history.htm

Glossary of Way Terms

The following glossary is quoted directly from Dr. John Juedes's Web site with his permission.[57] It has been edited for clarity and conciseness. Please take the time to read through these and know the ever-so-slightly warped take on common Christian words and practices.

* * * * *

ABUNDANT SHARING (and TITHING)
Every person owes God a tithe (10 percent) of his or her income; so, true giving begins after the "minimum payment" is made. The portion over the tithe is called "abundant sharing" and (with the tithe) is paid directly to TWI headquarters (at one time it meant giving this to people in need, not just to TWI). The unchanging "Law of Prosperity"

---

[57] John P. Juedes, "Way Jargon." In *Inside The Way International* [cited 5 May 2003]; available at http://www.empirenet.com/~messiah7 /quz_jargon.htm; INTERNET

is that the payment of one's "debt" of the tithe assures that the payer will not experience financial collapse, health problems, or accidents. Giving 11-15 percent is only sowing "sparingly," while giving 16 percent and up is sowing bountifully. Only those who give over 15 percent can attain wealth and receive abundance of revelation and inside knowledge of the Word. Leaders also advocate "plurality giving," determining one's needs and giving all income over that amount to TWI.

ADMINISTRATIONS
Wierwille adapted E. W. Bullinger's ultradispensationalism that divides history into seven administrations (dispensations). This system teaches that water baptism should no longer be practiced and that only the seven "church epistles" by the Apostle Paul are meant for Christians today, thereby placing little stock in the other fifty-nine biblical books.

ATHLETES OF THE SPIRIT
Martindale twists many meanings of Greek words in order to make all the military images in the New Testament (such as the armor of God in Ephesians 6) into athletic ones. Wierwille's successor starred in a dance production based on the concept.

BELIEVING (LAW OF BELIEVING)
One unchangeable law in the universe is that positive believing (being convinced that good things will happen) produces prosperous things in a person's life, while negative believing (fear) produces bad things. This has nothing to do with God, and works for believers and unbelievers alike. Wierwille claimed that one mother's fear that her boy would

be hurt was what caused him to be killed by an automobile. Wayers must not use words like *luck* or *fortunate*.

CHRISTEN-DUMB
All Christians who are not a part of TWI. Wierwille's replacement calls their churches "stained glass whorehouses." Wayers must not use Christian words like *Christmas* and *Easter*.

CHRIST IN YOU
The natural man is born with a body and soul, but not a spirit. When one is born, God creates a custom-made (human) spirit in him or her. It makes it possible for God to work with someone. The spirit is also called "Christ in you," "holy spirit," "inherent spiritual power," "power from on high," "spiritual abilities," and "the mystery." It is not Jesus Christ himself.

CONFRONTING (also called REPROVING, or ADMONISHING)
Leaders criticize and accuse those beneath them of error, mistakes, not using current jargon, and of not doing enough (or the proper things) for TWI. May include yelling, berating, screaming, or not allowing the subjects (victims?) to leave the room until leadership is finished convincing them to obey even small matters. This is a major theme in TWI ever since the power struggles that began after Wierwille's 1985 death, and is widely practiced and frequently taught.

CORPS (WAY CORPS)
TWI's three-year leadership training program paid for largely by donors the Corps students recruit. It includes Corps

(singles) and Family Corps (couples with children), which were trained at different locations when TWI was larger. Corps numbers are inflated because they count Junior (children) and Mini (small children) Corps. Recognized Corps status has been granted to longtime workers who didn't take the formal training. Since large numbers (perhaps 90 percent) of Corps grads left TWI, they have been categorized as Active, Emeritus, Alumni (in TWI but without Corps privileges), and Dropped (including DFAC [T], dropped during in-residence training, and DFAC [G], dropped after graduating).

CREATION OF THE HEAVENS AND EARTH
LCM's WAP class devotes several segments (much more time than it devotes to the life and teaching of Jesus Christ) to the creation, destruction, and recreation of the earth, attempting to integrate popular science with the Bible.

DEVIL SPIRITS
Invisible devil spirits (evil spirits) are repeatedly blamed for any doubts among Wayers or opposition to TWI.

FIGURES OF SPEECH
Some phrases in the Bible are to be taken figuratively, not literally, and are expressions designed to illustrate or emphasize a point (e.g., "God is a consuming fire"). These are widely known and understood, but TWI makes a big deal of highlighting technical names for different kinds of figures of speech, using material from E. W. Bullinger's huge book

Figures of Speech [58](one of several books by Bullinger which V. P. Wierwille plagiarized).

GREASE SPOT BY MIDNIGHT

Leaders may threaten followers of becoming harmed ("a grease spot") if they don't do what leaders require in a given situation; they may assert that any negative thing that happens to followers are because they were disobedient to leadership.

THE HOLY SPIRIT

The Holy Spirit (the first letters of which are capitalized) is another name for God the Father, as Bob is another name for Robert. God, who is Holy and is Spirit, is the Giver who gives his gift, holy spirit, to believers. (See "Christ in You" for a description of "holy spirit," which is not capitalized.)

HOMOSEXUALS (HOMOS)

Homosexuals are considered the most perverted of sinners, and are believed to be controlled by devil spirits. LCM's class teaches that a homosexual relationship between Eve and the devil was the first sin in the Garden of Eden, followed by Adam's acceptance of it.

HOUSEHOLD (HOUSEHOLD OF ZION)

Those who follow and obey Wierwille's successor. The "Corps Household" is a group of Corps grads that are obedient to Wierwille's successor; they are separate and superior to ordinary non-Corps believers. The "Trustee

---

[58] *Figures of Speech Used in the Bible* E.W. Bullinger Baker Book House, Grand Rapids, Michigan.

Household" is comprised of current and past trustees and their spouses who still follow the head of The Way.

JESUS CHRIST
Jesus is not God, but a perfect human that came into existence when the Father created sinless sperm and implanted it in Mary.

LAWS
God established immutable laws that govern human situations, such as the law of believing, law of prosperity, and law of tithing. Accordingly, what one does, believes, or confesses (affirms) causes either good or bad to come to him or her, depending on the degree to which he has carried out the laws.

LIES AND MALARKEY
Any criticism of TWI, even when entirely accurate and factual....reproves any sin committed by anyone by confronting the offender either on the spot or before twenty-four hours pass. See "Confronting."

LOVING OBEDIENCE
Obedience to every command or desire of TWI leadership without hesitation or question.

MEEK
[This means] having an attitude of "loving obedience."

THE MAN OF GOD
Wierwille and Martindale are the only real "men of God" whom God has appointed to lead believers (similar to Moses

or Jesus Christ). They get revelation directly from God, and followers must obey without question or hesitation.

MARKED TO AVOID

Or "purge, mark and avoid." The penalty for disobeying leadership or leaving TWI is that followers then "mark" (label them as erring) and "avoid" all contacts and conversations with them; this often prompts great stress in marriages, and sometimes divorce. TWI hoped this would result in a "clean household." The "cop-outs" who leave TWI on their own and those who are forced out by TWI leadership are both labeled "mark and avoid."

MOVE THE WORD

Getting paying students to take TWI's WAP class, as well as getting them to buy other classes and publications, and to support TWI. Christian activities such as distributing Bibles and translating the Bible into more languages are considered devilish (activity of the devil and his devil spirits), since they do not teach LCM's class WAP so people know how to read the Word.

OPERATE THE MANIFESTATIONS

Followers are taught how to speak in tongues, interpret tongues, and prophesy, and are expected to do so instantly when called on by a leader in any meeting.

PASSIONS OF INFAMY

A favorite Way phrase based on Romans 1:26, which indicates an illicit, unbridled lust. The most central of these is homosexuality, since it was the first sin of mankind in the Garden of Eden.

PRESENT TRUTH
The current teaching of Martindale, which all Wayers must follow, regardless of how much it differs from past TWI teaching. Leaders are told to teach from current issues of *The Way Magazine* and not to rely on TWI's past publications. This implies that past teaching and teachers were untrustworthy and that Wierwille's successor may introduce new teachings which must be accepted. This was necessary because most TWI teachers of the past accused Wierwille's successor of serious error and left to form their own groups, and because Wierwille's successor wants to shift allegiance from founder Wierwille to himself.

PROSPERITY (THE LAW OF PROSPERITY)
When believers give a tithe and more of their income, they will become financially prosperous. Way Corps Principle #4 is "Practice believing to bring material abundance to you and the ministry." Actually, few are financially prosperous because career advancement is to be sacrificed in order to serve TWI completely, and TWI has had to greatly reduce their material holdings in recent years as income has fallen.

PROTECTION OF THE HOUSEHOLD
If people do not obey and fellowship with current TWI leadership, they will be under the control of devil spirits and bad things will happen to them. Wierwille's successor wrote that if nuclear missiles exploded in America, "every community around you could disappear, but wherever the household of God stands strong, we remain unharmed." This is used to instill fear in followers in order to cause them to do what the leaders demand and to keep them from leaving TWI.

REMNANT
The small number of Wierwille's successor's devoted followers today, which are but a small portion of the number involved in TWI before V. P. Wierwille's death in 1985. To Wierwille's successor, this tiny "household of The Way" is the only place on earth where true believers fellowship and hear the accurate Word of God. They gather in "Twigs" (home groups) approved by TWI, in contrast to "Sticks," where ex-Wayers gather.

RENEWED MIND
Conformation of one's thoughts to the current teachings, terminology and practices promoted by TWI leadership

RESEARCH (KEYS TO BIBLICAL RESEARCH)
TWI sees itself as a research and teaching center rather than as a church. The old Power for Abundant Living class taught keys to biblical research that were simple and commonly known. The new WAP class de-emphasizes these. Many are used selectively in order to manipulate the Bible to make it appear to support TWI's preconceived theology. Although TWI denies it, leadership discourages personal research and instead emphasizes studying the research done in New Knoxville. Twig and other leaders are told to teach using the Sunday Service topics or current *Way Magazine* articles (older issues have too many articles by defectors).

SALT (KEEP THE SALT)
TWI uses ceremonies that use salt as a sign of commitment (e.g., Corps dedication, ordination, marriage). This is loosely

based on some ancient near eastern practices. Followers who actively support TWI and obey leadership are called "salted."

SENSES REALM
This ordinary human perception, judgment, and decision-making is criticized as being invalid and out of touch with God's will.

SPEAKING IN TONGUES (SIT)
SIT is the infallible evidence that a person has been born again. Believers are told to SIT constantly after being taught how to do so by Way leaders.

STATUS (includes STANDING)
TWI classifies its present and past followers into five categories. "Standing" followers are active in TWI activities, obey TWI leaders and tithe and/or abundantly share finances to TWI. They may receive mail and buy bookstore items, *The Way Magazine*, and tapes. "Inactive" are willing to be active in TWI but are unable to due to distance or incarceration. They may buy TWI items. "Not Standing" are people who have taken Way classes and are not willing to come to TWI activities even though they are not antagonistic toward TWI. TWI will not send them mail or sell bookstore items to them. Wayers on "Probation" are not allowed in TWI fellowships for a period of time because they have not yet fulfilled requirements TWI leaders have set for them (such as getting out of debt or moving closer to leadership). Those who are "Mark and Avoid" cannot receive TWI mail, bookstore items, magazines, or tapes, and are not allowed into TWI fellowships. When people call or write TWI, their names are

checked against the status list, which determines whether or not the inquiries will be answered.

SUNDAY NIGHT SERVICE (or SUNDAY TEACHING SERVICE)
Wayers are expected to attend the weekly hymn and teaching service if they live within 250 miles of New Knoxville, or (if they live farther away) to have a live telephone hookup, or to buy the weekly tape subscription. When the time was moved to earlier in the day as a result of complaints from those who had a long drive home late at night, the name was changed to STS.

TITHING DEBT
Wayers are expected to give a minimum of 10 percent of their income to TWI; this is considered a debt to God, not a gift freely offered. Leaders may check to see if followers have continued to give 10 percent, and may require "back tithes" when they are behind.

TRADITION
Any teaching or practice that differs from those of TWI, even if it is more biblically accurate or chronologically much newer than anything held by TWI.

WAY DISCIPLES
Devout followers of TWI who are assigned to certain cities to recruit new Wayers for six month periods; LCM established this program to replace the Word over the World Ambassadors, who did the same for one-year terms. They must be graduates of the WAP Advanced class.

WAY OF ABUNDANCE AND POWER (WAP)
A videotaped, twenty-four-segment class taught by LCM in order to indoctrinate new recruits in the teachings and practices of TWI; it has three separate levels, Foundational (twenty-four segments), Intermediate (twelve segments), and Advanced. A higher level of commitment to TWI is required in order to take each higher class; it replaced Wierwille's Power for Abundant Living class.

WAY TREE
The hierarchical chain of command beginning at the top with the root (President and Trustees in New Knoxville), Trunk (countries), Limb (state or multi-state), Branch (regional), Twig Area (group of home fellowships); leaders require complete obedience and approval of all activities. V. P. Wierwille initiated the Tree about 1970 in order to control the formerly independent fellowships affiliated with TWI across the country. The three Trustees, [names withheld], have absolute power, are placed in office for indefinite terms, and are accountable to no one.

Splinter Groups

It is not known exactly when The Way was founded, but it is believed to be somewhere between 1957 and 1958. New Knoxville, Ohio, is the current headquarters for the main movement. However, there are other splinter groups that have developed due to controversy previous to and following the death of Wierwille on May 20, 1985. Apparently, an assemblage involving all of the believers from the state (Limb) of South Carolina, and a majority of the Limb of Washington, D.C., have started their own home-based organizations.[59] Other large groups include Way of New York, currently called Christian Biblical Council, located in Latham, New York. Additional apparent splinter groups are as follows:

---

[59] Joel A. MacCollam, *The Way of Victor Paul Wierwille* (Downers Grove, IL.: Intervarsity Press, 1978).

Christian Educational Services (CES), which incorporated in the fall of 1988 in Indianapolis,[60] appears to be one of the largest of the splinter groups. These ex-Wayers were formally known as American Fellowship Services. The people who run this splinter group were all once highly visible members of the original Wierwille's Way, or in leadership and teaching positions. CES teachings are basically the same as Wierwille's; however, "corrections" have been made because his teachings were not "always biblically accurate." They are still non-Trinitarian, which is one of the primary reasons this cult and the splinter groups associated with Wierwille's teachings can be so damaging to the new, unsuspecting recruit.

In a phone interview with a CES leader[61] who was formerly with The Way International Research Department, I asked if he believed Wierwille was a "man of God." Throughout this conversation, despite the fact he was the author of an article concerning sexual misconduct by Wierwille and Way leadership, he defended this man as "leading him to the Lord Jesus Christ." It was due to this research paper that this man and several others who aided him in this endeavor were fired from the staff of TWI in the late '80s. An afterword to this paper reveals that anyone in TWI found reading the article would never be promoted in the TWI leadership beyond that of the lowest level. The following excerpt was taken from a public domain Web site. It appears at the end of the paper

---

[60] John P. Juedes, "The Way Tree is Splintering." In *Christian Research Institute Journal* [cited 5 May 2003]; available at http://iclnet.org/pub/resources/text/cri/cri-jrnl/web/crj0029a.html; INTERNET.

[61] Schoenheit, John, telephone interview by the author, November 2000.

entitled "Research Paper on Adultery," under the heading "Background of the paper."[62]

> *My story (short version): In the spring of 1986 a girl came to me and said she had had sexual intercourse with Dr. Wierwille. I had no reason to doubt her as we were friends and she "had her head on her shoulders" in life. I started asking around to girls I knew always got to ride on the motor coach, fly on Ambassador 1,[63] get "back room" duty instead of housekeeping or grounds [duty] etc. Lo and behold, I talked to many women that were very candid about their sexual relations with leadership.*

> *Perhaps the most disturbing thing about those months was the developing picture was that this was not just practical sin based on lust but rather was sin based on wrong doctrine—many of the people involved thought it was okay with God. In fact, all of the "reasons" that I wrote about in my appendix came out of the mouths of women I talked to. I would ask them why they thought it was okay or why they were told it was okay and those*

---

[62] Schoenheit, John, "Research Paper on Adultery." In *Beyond The Way International Document Archive at SwiftLynx* [cited 5 May 2003]; available at http://www.swiftlynx.com/beyondTheWayInternational/Adultery.htm; INTERNET.

[63] The private plane Wierwille purchased with members' tithing and "abundant sharing."

were the reasons I got, so that is why I answered those specific questions.

In the midst of interviewing the women I suspected might have had sexual relations with leadership, I had three different women tell me I would be killed if I tried to stop it. The first time I thought it was a totally stupid thing, but by the third one I really stopped and thought about it. David had Uriah killed for the same reason. To protect my work I sent it to about 7 people I knew and trusted (I do not remember the exact number or all the people now) sealed in an envelope inside an envelope with instructions to "go public" if I ended up dead. I told them that the paper was going to be sent up proper channels, and not to share the work with others. As you know, The Way had strict guidelines for handling research, and at that time I had been in the system even though I was beginning to have doubts bout the integrity of the leadership. I handed the paper in to Walter Cummins in later September. It just sat on his desk. One of the people I had given a copy to had been hurt by the sex stuff and really wanted it to "make an impact."...

On October 23rd I was "released" from The Way by order of [name withheld]. It was a Friday....it was...stated that the paper had devil spirits and anyone who read it became possessed. In time I hooked up with [names withheld], and some others and CES

[Christian Educational Services] was born. It took awhile for the smoke to clear, but when it did all that was left of us was [names withheld] and myself, and we have been together ever since. The Lord has been leading us, and now I think we are turning out some really first-class stuff.[64]

This "stuff" they are turning out is anti-Trinitarian, anti-Catholic, and in passionate defense of Wierwille. Be *very* wary of this group and others described here.

These are several things to look for when avoiding Way-affiliated splinter groups: Be suspicious if they use the term *believer* for people who agree in doctrine with them. This is a often used description of anyone who has taken the PFAL class. I have gone to probably over one hundred different "believer" Web sites and most have links to other "believers." Without too many exceptions, these people are forming or have formed their own groups that adhere to Wierwille teachings.

Be aware that they will probably be anti-Trinitarian, or, as some prefer, "non-Trinitarian." You will find, however, most are vigorously *anti*-Trinitarian, with the emphasis on the *anti*.

Other issues to be aware of:

---

[64] The full research paper, now public domain, can be found at: Schoenheit, John, "Research Paper on Adultery." In *Beyond The Way International Document Archive at SwiftLynx* [cited 5 May 2003]; available at http://www.swiftlynx.com/beyondTheWayInternational/Adultery.htm; INTERNET.

Wierwille followers will also defend him as a "man of God." In my research of these splinter groups, and there are hundreds, they most likely will worship in a home and will commonly have "teaching" ministries or "research" ministries. They will shy away from calling their organization a church and will generally be anti-Catholic and anti-Jewish.

Below is a partial list of these splinter groups. In some cases I included their URL or e-mail contact. In most cases, I did not as these Web sites often change.

- Ex-CES Followers Web Site
  http://ex-ces.faithweb.com/index.html
- Biblical Research and Teaching—Artios
- The Prayer Room
- Home Bible Fellowship
- The Bereans
- Cortwright Fellowship Homepage
- Christian Family Fellowship
- Word Centered Productions/Glad Magazine
  http://www.wordcentered.com/
- Center for the Advancement of First Century Christianity
- Ministry of Reconciliation (MOR)
- Bible Center (Formally Der Weg)

Another large group, reportedly the second largest, is the Pacific West Fellowship, headed by a man who was once a Limb and Region Coordinator.[65]

The Way is highly structured. Wierwille used the tree to designate the levels of the organization. At the base, or roots, is the president/board of directors. After Wierwille's death, a new president, handpicked by Wierwille, took over, causing

---

[65] Harold J. Berry, *The Way International: What They Believe* (Lincoln, NE: Back to the Bible, 1992).

much of the inner turmoil currently within the group. In September of 2000, Wierwille's replacement, Martindale, had to step down as president of TWI due to allegations of sexual misconduct. A lawsuit was settled and others are pending as of this writing against him and The Way International.

Recommended Reading

Pile, Lawrence A. "Binding up the Broken: How to Help Victims of Cults and Spiritual Abuse." *Ministries Today*, May/June 1994, Cover story.

Anderson, Neil T. *The Bondage Breaker.* Harvest House, Eugene, OR 1997.

Adair, James A. and Ted Miller. *Escape From Darkness.* : SP Publications, Inc., Victor Books, Wheaton, IL 1982.

McDowell, Josh and Don Stewart. *Handbook of Today's Religions.* Nashville, TN: Thomas Nelson, 1992.

Tucker, Bruce. *Twisting the Truth.* Bloomington, MN: Bethany House, 1987.

Enroth, Ronald. *Recovering from Churches that Abuse.* Zondervan Publishing House, Grand Rapids, MI 1994.

Wellspring Retreat and Resource Center, comp. *The Way International.* Albany, OH: Wellspring Retreat and Resource Center, http://wellspringretreat.org/

Ankerberg, John and John Weldon. *Cult Watch: What You Need to Know about Spiritual Deception.* Eugene, OR Harvest House, 1991.

Michaelsen, Johanna. *The Beautiful Side of Evil. :* Caroline House Publishing, Honesdale, PA 1984. This should be mandatory reading for every Christian.

Lee, Richard and Ed Hindson. *Angels of Deceit: The Masterminds behind Religious Deceptions.* Eugene, OR: Harvest House, 1993.

Martin, Walter. *The Kingdom of the Cults.* Bloomington, MN: Bethany House, 1985.

Singer, Margaret T. and Janja Lalich *Cults in Our Midst: The Hidden Menace in Our Everyday Lives.* Reprint ed. San Francisco, CA: Jossey-Bass, 1995.

Kahler, Karl. *The Cult That Snapped: A Journey Into The Way International.* Los Gatos, CA: , 1999.

References

Ahearn, Lorraine. "Mind Control Called the Way of the Way." *The Capital*, 2 April 1986, Front page continued on Page 12 Col. 2, April 2, 1986 The Capital, Annapolis, MD.

Berry, Harold J. *The Way International: What They Believe.* Lincoln, NE: Back to the Bible, 1992.

Craig, Shawn and Don Koch. "In Christ Alone." *The Michael English Album.* Performed by Michael English. Paragon Music Corp. 1990.

Juedes, John P. "The Way Tree is Splintering." In *Christian Research Institute Journal* [cited 5 May 2003]; available at http://iclnet.org/pub/resources/text/cri/cri-jrnl/web/crj00 29a.html; INTERNET.

"Way Jargon." In *Inside The Way International* [cited 5 May 2003]; available at http://www.empirenet.com/~messiah7 /quz_jargon.htm; INTERNET.

http://www.empirenet.com/~messiah7/quiz_ipikepk.htm

Kahler, Karl. *The Cult That Snapped: A Journey into The Way International.* Los Gatos, CA: n.p.1999.

Wapakonete (OH) Daily News, 27 April 2000.

MacCollam, Joel A. *The Way of Victor Paul Wierwille.* Downers Grove, IL: Intervarsity Press, 1978.

McDowell, Josh and Don Stewart. *Handbook of Today's Religions.* Nashville, TN: Thomas Nelson, 1992.

Schoenheit, John. "Research Paper on Adultery." In *Beyond The Way International Document Archive at SwiftLynx* [cited 5 May 2003]; available at http://www.swiftlynx. com/beyondTheWayInternational/Adultery.htm; INTERNET.

Singer, Margaret T. and Janja Lalich. *Cults in Our Midst: The Hidden Menace in Our Everyday Lives.* Reprint ed. San Francisco, CA: Jossey-Bass, 1995.

Whiteside, Elena S. *The Way: Living in Love.* 2d ed. New Knoxville, OH: American Christian Press, 1972.

Wierwille, Victor Paul. *Jesus Christ is Not God.* New Knoxville, OH: American Christian Press, 1984.

Wierwille, Victor Paul. *Power for Abundant Living.* New Knoxville, OH: American Christian Press, 1984.

Acknowledgments

There are several people to whom I owe a heartfelt thank you.

Dr. John Weldon, a published author who has also co-written many books with John Ankerberg, was the first professional I called when I realized I had used up six years of my life in a cult. My shame and humiliation left me reeling. He not only took my phone call, but many subsequent phone calls after that. His care and concern were keys to my recovery. His encouragement to write about my experiences eventually led me to writing this book (along with a very strong nudging from God).

I have to express how grateful I am to Michael English for getting me through the final stage of recovery. It was his voice that God used to reach my confused and hurting heart. I was so beaten down, and so terribly drained that it seemed the battle might be too much. God gave me Michael's music and used his voice to not only pierce the darkness, but to give me hope—a rare commodity for me at that time. The words, the music, and that anointed voice reached deep into the very core of me and I began to see a light. It was as if I had chosen the songs Michael was to sing to uplift my very tired spirit. I rejoice in God's mercy and goodness. Thank you, Michael, from the bottom of my heart for heeding his call.

I must thank Pastor Mike Bartholomew for his tender care and patience as he guided me out of the cult teachings of The Way. His constant prayers and the time he continually took to shepherd me out of the cult teachings is something I will never forget. What a great man of God he was and still is.

I wish also to give thanks to each of my lovely children. They are all grown up now, and a constant source of joy and wonder to me. I can't believe God has blessed us with such tremendous examples of his love.

I need to thank my mother. She raised me, as a struggling single parent, along with my grandmother. Their examples showed me that hard work and discipline are not only very important, but also rewarding. They sacrificed so much to give me a roof over my head and ultimately to give me a four-year education. Mom, I always knew I was loved, no matter what our struggles. We did it together, the three of us, and made it through! Thank you for all the sacrifices you made and thank you for loving me.

For the wisest woman I have ever known, my Gramma. She's no longer alive, but she remains very much alive in my heart. Hardly a day will go by when I do not think of her or remember a life lesson she taught me. What a pillar of strength! What a woman!

I must also acknowledge my 7th grade English teacher, Harold Qualters. He told me I could write, that I had "talent" and that I should continue to write. He planted the seed and gave me the confidence in myself that I sorely lacked in those days. He believed in me, and it is due to his encouragement that I began to write and love to write to this day."

Last, but not least, I must acknowledge my editor, Deb Austin. There is positively no way this story could have been told without her professional help. She worked on my story as if it were her own. I was constantly amazed at how she took the rough edges of my testimony and molded it into what you hold in your hands. She is a gem, and a very talented professional whom I am now blessed to call my friend.

Thank you, Jesus, for the special people you've placed in my life. I am better for knowing them and growing better for knowing you.

About the Author

Carol Van Drie is a published writer and an army wife of over twenty-three years. She currently resides in Carlisle, Pennsylvania with her beloved husband, Mark; and her three children, Amber, Allison, and Alex. She shares her home with three Yorkshire terriers, Taffy, Buckley, and Indy; along with her Persian cat, Ellie May.

In her spare time Carol sings in her church choir and a woman's Christian group called Joyful Noise. She volunteers for various animal rescue groups and will sometimes be a foster parent for homeless dogs and cats until they can be placed in a permanent home. She currently is a freelance correspondent for a local newspaper and is looking forward to what might be her last move as an army wife to Lansing, Michgian in the summer of June 2004.

Carol speaks publicly about cults and false or destructive religious organizations, and continues to minister to cult victims and their families through her Web site, Obadiah Ministries:
http://users.churchserve.com/pa/obadiahministries/.